NEEDLEWORK FROM NATURE

NEEDLEWORK FROM NATURE

A World of Inspirational Charted Designs
for needlepoint and counted cross-stitch

DEBORAH ANN MURPHY

Charts by Beverley Zadikoff

Fleming H. Revell Company
Old Tappan, New Jersey

Illustrations and accompanying captions from pp. 47–51 of
CAROLYN AMBUTER'S COMPLETE BOOK OF
NEEDLEPOINT (Thomas Y. Crowell)
Copyright © 1972 by Carolyn Ambuter
Reprinted by permission of Harper & Row, Publishers, Inc.

Library of Congress Cataloging-in-Publication Data

Murphy, Deborah Ann.
  Needlework from nature.

  Bibliography: p.
  Includes index.
  1. Needlework—Patterns. 2. Decoration and
ornament.
  I. Title.
TT753.M87 1987   746.44   87-20559
ISBN 0-8007-1559-4

Copyright © 1987 by Deborah Ann Murphy
Published by the Fleming H. Revell Company
Old Tappan, New Jersey 07675
Printed in the United States of America

TO Gene and Patrick

With special thanks to all the stitchers who worked on my samples

To Pamela Landfear, for all her help
To Susan Kolodny, for her expertise

And above all to Beverley Zadikoff,
without whose meticulousness, enthusiasm, and sense of humor,
this book would not have been possible.

CONTENTS

INTRODUCTION

Recently, when I accepted the commission of a church in my community to design cushions and kneelers for them, I was swept into a world of Christian symbolism richer and more eloquent than anything I could have dreamed existed. I decided to use a modified millefleurs theme, in which animals, plants, birds, and insects would convey Christian meaning in diverse profusion.

As I began to search out suitable subjects, I became immersed in a wealth of material, but found very little of it easily adaptable to needlework. No book combined designs to stitch with informative text. So, using my research, I decided to write a book that others could use for projects in the church or home and that expressed Christian concepts in designs from nature. *Needlework From Nature* is a collection of needlepoint designs of animals, plants, birds, and insects that convey Christian meaning and are adapted for needlepoint or counted cross-stitch. The symbolic meanings of the designs precede the detailed charts. As sources for the meaning of each entry I have used literary and historical works, reference texts, the Bible, tapestry, art, and architecture; a bibliography at the back of the book provides more information on them.

In some cases early Christians adapted ancient secular symbols to convey new meanings. Other symbols come directly from the Bible and are as recognizable to contemporary Christians as they were to those of the first century A.D. A third group have evolved more recently as lay expressions of Christian faith and devotion based on the familiar surroundings of everyday life. While interpretations may vary and are sometimes even contradictory, all are richly evocative and fascinating.

For each chart I have indicated colors and yarns. In Chapter 1, I recommend specific yarns and discuss their color ranges.

In addition the first chapter will help individuals or groups take a project from initial conception through techniques and materials to finishing. Diagrams are provided for stitching, and guidelines show you how to figure the shapes and sizes of various projects. The alphabetical index on page 95 can be used to pick appealing or appropriate subjects.

Chapter 2 includes designs for animals, real or imagined, such as the *lion* and *griffin*. In Chapter 3 are birds and insects: both mythical ones, such as the *phoenix*, and ones as familiar as the *butterfly*. Plants are included in Chapter 4 and borders and background designs in Chapter 5. The borders, based on traditional shapes in Christian artwork, architecture, and wood carving, can be used interchangeably. They can also be used for boxing strips around cushions.

I hope the reader will be inspired by the work of other diligent stitchers and will be moved to use these designs in new arrangements that will reflect creative Christian devotion. I also hope this book will be an informative and inspiring collection of fascinating symbols. Finally, I encourage the eager and the curious to use my bibliography for further exploration of the rich and varied world of Christian symbols.

1
PLANNING YOUR PROJECT

Before starting a design, you should plan a project by deciding where it will go, what its dimensions will be, what stitches you want to use, how you want it finished, and who will finish it. Make all these decisions before taking a single stitch, especially if the finished piece is to fit a piece of furniture or architectural space.

Know where your needlepoint or cross-stitch project will go first, because the light in that area, the size of the room, and the other furniture in it will influence all the elements.

If you wish to fit a needlepoint project into furniture or a specific space, measure the area very carefully with a metal tape and note it. For chair seats that will be upholstered into wood, add one inch all around to compensate for padding. For knife-edge and boxed cushions, add three-eighths inch to one-half inch beyond the design area, for seam allowance. If measuring a space for church kneelers that will be placed side by side, subtract one inch per cushion (in width and depth) to allow for the bulging that will occur when they are used. For rugs, add three-quarters of an inch all around, which will later be turned under or bound. For risers and runners, stitch the exact measurement, unless they are to be padded, in which case add one-half inch all around. For bellpulls and wall hangings, stitch the exact measurement or one-eighth inch to three-eighths inch less, if velvet cording will be used in finishing. For framed pieces, consider that a frame and liner or mat will take up additional space. The size of your project is determined by its ultimate destination. Throw pillows for a sofa might be as small as eight inches across or as large as eighteen inches; cushions that must fit into or onto furniture must conform exactly to the allotted space.

Choosing Colors

Having decided on the dimensions of your project, you should now consider the colors. Your choices will be based on what is available, how it will wear, and how its colors will look. Check local shops for first quality 100 percent wool yarn for needlepointing. In my samples I have used three-ply persian, Medicis, coton perle, and floss. Select small amounts of the colors you are considering and see how they look stitched in a chosen setting. It is surprising how colors can darken (persian) or lighten (perle) when they are stitched. The ambient light will influence the colors, too.

Your colors should blend with or complement the existing colors in your home or church. In your yarn palette include at least two distinctly contrasting colors and two to five values in each of the dominant hues you pick. Do not be afraid to add accents that are opposite in the color wheel to the colors that predominate. (*See* Illustration 1.)

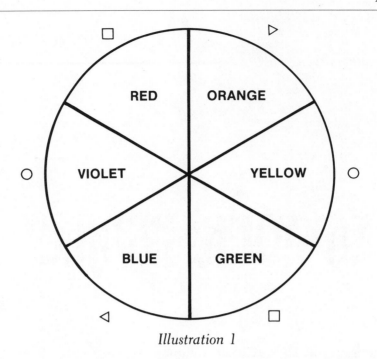

Illustration 1

At home consider the color of your carpet, the walls, drapery and upholstery fabrics. In a church, be sure to consider the colors of the stained glass, wood, stone, and existing needlework; and do so at various times of the day, to see how the changing light affects the established colors.

Choosing a Subject

To decide on the subject matter, rely on your instinct and the atmosphere of the location you have chosen. Look at the art and handwork there—what are their motifs? Notice the colors, shapes, and styles of the furniture and architecture. Are there rounded corners? Hexagonal shapes? Do designs already incorporated into the room have Christian meaning? Are there some distinctive shapes to copy or modify? It is far more intriguing to stitch a project that relates directly to the space it will occupy than one randomly selected.

The shapes and subject matter of the room's decor will help you decide on a theme. If there are no decorative shapes and forms you can readily interpret, rely on a more subjective approach, using favorite flowers, plants, animals, or birds—or consider birth-month flowers.

On the other hand, you might choose a Christian concept such as *humility* or *purity* and find the subject that depicts it. Many concepts have several entries. You may want to use them individually or in combination with other symbols. The Index will provide you with this information.

For a church project, if there are no predominant themes, consult with your group and consider such sources of design as the name of the church, its location or age, special events that have been observed there, a special tradition your church continues, or favorite flowers, birds, or plants. In *Needlework From Nature* you will find designs that have special significance for you or your group.

When you have decided on the themes, find the appropriate charts, and following the color suggestions, use the colors you have selected. Before stitching, decide how many designs to include in your piece. A single flower might eloquently depict the meaning you intend. Or several flowers accompanied by a bird or insect could express several ideas. Perhaps a simple shape could be repeated in subtle colors to make a patterned background. Chapter 5 provides borders that can be used around patterns or on their own as boxing strips, luggage-rack straps, belts, or bellpulls.

Many factors will govern the number of symbolic designs used in each project, including the skill of the stitcher or stitchers, the surrounding decor, and the size of the finished piece. If you decide to use more than one chart, be sure to calculate the design size on the mesh size you have chosen. Stitch counts are provided with each chart. To figure out the finished size of a given needlepoint mesh, divide the stitch count by the mesh size. For example, a chart of 192 stitches by 214 stitches will be 19.2 inches by 21.4 inches on 10 mesh and 10.7 inches by 11.9 inches on 18 mesh. Use the Evenweave Computation Chart below to verify your calculations.

EVENWEAVE COMPUTATION CHART
(TO DETERMINE DESIGN AREA ONLY)

(add 4"-6" to design area figure before cutting fabric)

STITCH COUNT IN LENGTH & WIDTH

THREAD COUNT PER INCH	20	25	30	35	40	45	50	55	60	65	70	75	80	85	90	95	100
6	3⅜	4⅛	5	5⅞	6¾	7½	8⅜	9⅛	10	10⅞	11¾	12½	13⅜	14⅛	15	15⅞	16¾
8	2½	3⅛	3¾	4⅜	5	5⅝	6¼	6⅞	7½	8⅛	8¾	9⅜	10	10⅝	11¼	11⅞	12½
11	1⅞	2¼	2¾	3⅛	3⅝	4⅛	4½	5	5½	5⅞	6⅜	6⅞	7¼	7¾	8¼	8⅝	9⅛
13	1½	2	2⅜	2⅞	3⅛	3½	3⅞	4¼	4⅝	5	5⅜	5½	6⅛	6½	6⅞	7⅜	7⅝
14	1⅜	1⅞	2⅛	2½	2⅞	3⅛	3½	3⅞	4¼	4⅝	5	5⅜	5¾	6	6⅜	6¾	7⅛
18	1⅛	1⅜	1⅝	2	2¼	2½	2¾	3	3⅜	3⅝	3⅞	4¼	4½	4¾	5	5¼	5½
22	⅞	⅛	1⅜	1⅝	1⅞	2⅛	2¼	2½	2¾	3	3⅛	3⅜	3⅝	3⅞	4⅛	4⅜	4½
27	¾	⅞	1⅛	1⅜	1½	1⅝	1⅞	2⅛	2¼	2⅜	2½	2⅝	2⅞	3⅛	3⅜	3½	3⅝
30	⅝	⅞	1	1⅛	1¼	1½	1⅝	1⅞	2	2⅛	2⅜	2½	2⅝	2⅞	3	3⅛	3¼

THREAD COUNT PER INCH	105	110	115	120	125	130	135	140	150	160	170	180	190	200	210	220	230	240	250
6	17½	18⅜	19⅛	20	20⅞	21¾	22½	23⅜	25	26⅝	28⅜	30	31⅝	33⅜	35	36⅝	38⅜	40	41⅝
8	13⅛	13¾	14⅜	15	15⅝	16¼	16⅞	17½	18¾	20	21¼	22½	23¾	25	26¼	27½	28¾	30	31¼
11	9½	10	10½	10⅞	11⅜	11⅞	12¼	12¾	13⅝	14½	15½	16⅜	17¼	18¼	19⅛	20	21	21⅞	22¾
13	8	8½	8⅞	9¼	9⅝	10	10⅜	10¾	11½	12⅜	13⅛	13⅞	14⅝	15⅜	16⅛	17	17⅝	18½	19¼
14	7½	7⅞	8¼	8½	8⅞	9¼	9⅞	10	10¾	11½	12⅛	12⅞	13½	14¼	15	15¾	16⅜	17⅛	17⅞
18	5⅞	6⅛	6⅜	6⅝	7	7¼	7½	7¾	8⅜	8⅞	9⅜	10	10½	11⅛	11⅝	12¼	12¾	13	13⅞
22	4¾	5	5¼	5½	5⅜	5⅞	6⅛	6⅜	6⅞	7¼	7¾	8⅛	8⅝	9⅛	9½	10	10½	11	11⅜
27	3⅞	4⅛	4¼	4½	4⅝	4¾	5	5⅛	5⅝	5⅞	6⅜	6¾	7	7⅜	7¾	8⅛	8⅝	8⅞	9¼
30	3½	3⅝	3⅞	4	4⅛	4⅜	4½	4⅝	5	5⅜	5⅝	6	6⅜	6⅝	7	7⅛	7⅜	8	8⅜

Evenweave Computation Chart reprinted by special permission of Designs by Gloria & Pat, Inc. © 1986.

When you plan to combine designs, use transparent graph paper to count the outline of each subject, then arrange and rearrange the pieces of paper to decide on the best composition or grouping of elements. By using transparent paper, you will be able to see all the designs as they overlap and adjust them until they look balanced. It is much easier to replace and retape paper patterns than it is to stitch and rip!

Choosing Stitches

When you decide on what type of stitch or stitches to use, consider how much wear the piece will get. Decorative stitches do not hold up as well as tent stitches and should be used only on projects that will be subjected to little or no wear. I recommend basketweave for church projects that will be walked on, kneeled on, or sat on. (For more information on stitches see pages 17–23).

Consider using a frame, when you plan a project. Work done on a frame will stay straight, when properly stitched, and a frame may also keep your project manageable. Stretcher-bar or roller-bar frames may be used, depending on the size of the piece.

Pieces not worked on a frame need not become severely distorted (stitching techniques are discussed later in this chapter). Tent stitches properly worked distort less than diagonal decorative stitches, and vertical or horizontal stitches distort virtually not at all. On the other hand, a competent finisher can block most distorted work.

Decide on Finishing

Before beginning your project, decide on how it will be finished and who will finish it. Will you stitch a boxing strip or use fabric? Will you use cording? What color will surround the piece and will it be fabric or wood? Should it be done in sections? Will tassels be made of extra yarn? Answering these and other questions before you start stitching will help you avoid the disappointment of completing a piece that cannot be properly finished. All stitched work should be surrounded by two inches of unworked canvas (in addition to seam measurements) so that it can be handled easily when blocked and finished. Consult a finisher or upholsterer for answers to questions about finishing.

I recommend professional finishing, especially for church projects. If, however, you decide to have a nonprofessional do the finishing, be sure to experiment first with a small sample of the same canvas and yarn you will use in your final project. Home sewing machines often do not have the power to stitch through the many layers of fabric, yarn, and canvas that are required to finish a project. Even handwork can entail some surprises. Above all, have your piece properly blocked. The most beautiful finishing technique can never make a crooked piece straight.

If you wish to have a piece professionally finished, consult with the finisher as you plan the project. This will insure that the correct amount of stitching has been done. Also confirm a price and the amount of time the finisher will need. While both factors may change, if your project takes a long time to complete, at least you will have an idea and will not be shocked or disappointed by the cost or time. This is particularly important for pieces being stitched for certain dates.

Find a good finisher by looking at finished projects in shops, in the homes of friends, or in churches. Be sure the finisher has handled needlepoint. The best upholsterers may not be able to cope with the special care (including proper cleaning and blocking) that needlepoint requires. Do not rely solely on recommendations. Be sure to see finished samples.

Now you are ready to stitch!

Materials and Techniques

Needlepoint Canvas

There are various types of needlepoint canvas available in several widths and mesh sizes. For most of these projects I have used *Zweigart mono.* It is a single weave, heavy duty, sized canvas with a rounded thread that will not shred yarn and will wear well. It is available in 18, 17, 16, 14, 13, 12, and 10 meshes, in 40 and 54 inch widths. Numbers 17 and 13 are available in tan, which is useful in counted work, because it does not show (as white canvas may) between stitches of medium or dark colors. Tan canvas will subtly darken white and the palest pastels, but will not otherwise influence the yarn colors used. In white 18, 16, 14, 13, 12, and 10 are available.

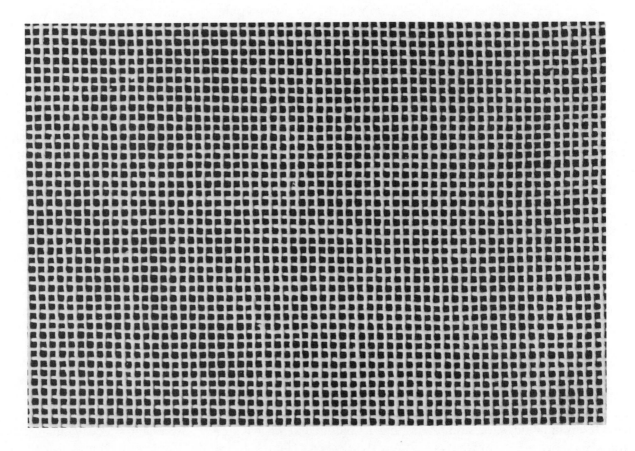

Zweigart Mono

Interlock canvas, in which the weft strands are interlocked at each intersection of the warp (rather than woven) is useful for some projects, because it does not shift or slide. However, the threads of interlocking canvas are flatter and lighter weight than mono and may shred the yarn slightly as it is stitched, leave less body, and may not wear as well.

Interlock Canvas

Penelope canvas, in which the double weft strands are interlocked with a single warp strand, is useful for projects in which petit point areas need to be worked, but otherwise is similar to interlocking canvas and may be confusing to the novice.

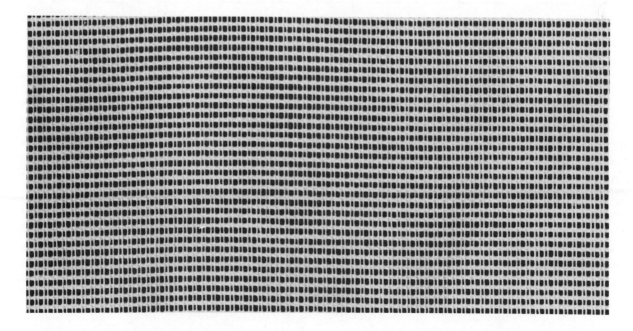

When planning your layout on canvas, be sure the selvage edges are on the left and right, rather than top and bottom, and that you stitch the front of your work on the side of the canvas that was rolled on the inside of the bolt. This will ensure that you will work the design *with* the grain and on the *right* side.

The mesh size, of the canvas will determine the finished size of the charted work in this book. Remember that when choosing a mesh size, and consider, too, that the smaller holes (18 through 16) are harder to see and will not wear as well as larger meshes (14 through 10).

Yarn

Your canvas choice will also influence the yarn you choose—all yarns do not fit well into every mesh. In my samples I have used Paternayan Persian, a three-ply 100 percent wool yarn that is softly lustrous and springy and comes in more than four hundred colors; Broder Medicis, a single-ply, very fine 100 percent wool with a matte finish, which is extremely even and easy to use and comes in a palette of over one hundred colors; DMC Perle Coton, 100 percent cotton yarn in a single twisted ply, which has a soft sheen, is available in two sizes (number 3 and number 5) and two hundred colors; and DMC Embroidery Floss, a six-ply 100 percent cotton with a subtle luster, which is available in skeins of twenty-five meters and in over three hundred colors (many of which are also available in number 3 and number 5 perle). Persian can be worked on 18 through 10 mesh by increasing the number of ply used from a single strand to three strands, although it is awkward on 16 or 14 mesh. Medicis can be used in all mesh sizes, although it requires at least six strands for number 10, which makes it expensive. Number 5 perle is used on mesh sizes 18 and 16; number 3 on 14 through 10. Embroidery floss is usually used in needlepoint in combination with other strands of wool, or on 18 and 16, using six ply and four ply respectively.

Suggested Number of Strands

	Canvas Mesh Count						Aida Cloth Count				Linen Fiber Count		
	10	12	13	14	16	18	11	14	18	22	26	30	32
Persian	3	2	2	2	1	1							
Medici	6	5	5	4	3	2							
Floss	12	10	10	8	6	6	3 or 4	3 or 2	2	1	2	1	1
DMC #5					1	1	1						
DMC #3	1	1	1	1									

Yarn colors are not necessarily colorfast, especially in cotton. Discuss your yarn choices with a knowledgeable person in your local shop before deciding on the fibers for your project. *Be sure* to check for colorfastness before blocking or have your piece dry blocked. Recent environmental protection laws have mandated that some components in the dyeing process of yarns be eliminated and safer substitutes used; this means more than ever that some colors will run when wet.

Be sure to purchase an ample amount of yarn. To estimate the quantity, stitch a sample square area on your chosen mesh and note the amount of yarn it took. Then, guessing the number of square inches per color, estimate the number of strands per color. Verify your estimate with your shop and add an allowance for ripping, variations in tension, and frequent color changes if necessary (stopping and starting often takes up extra yarn). Be sure to inform the salesperson about the stitches you plan to use. Basketweave takes more yarn than continental, and some decorative stitches (vertical) require more ply than tent stitches for the same canvas.

Always buy a generous amount of your background color so you will not run out and be unable to purchase the same dye lot. Most stores have a return policy for extra yarn; you should find out about it at the time of purchase.

Before purchasing the quantities you will need, be sure to stitch small amounts of the colors you have decided on to see how they look in their chosen location. The lighting of the shop may vary enough from your living room or church that you will need to adjust the colors.

Start Stitching!

Your next step is to start stitching! When working from a chart, find the middle of the canvas by folding it vertically and horizontally, and begin in the center of the chart. I have indicated the center of each side of the chart with small arrows (↓ ←). Follow them to the middle. By starting there, you will avoid inadvertently running off the edge because of a mistake in counting. A magnetic board and bar (line keeper) will help you read charted work by assisting your eye in finding the area you are counting as you look up and down from your work.

Each square in the charts represents a stitch, and colors are indicated by different graphic symbols in each box. The color suggestions accompanying each chart may be modified to reflect your palette of yarn colors.

Tent Stitch

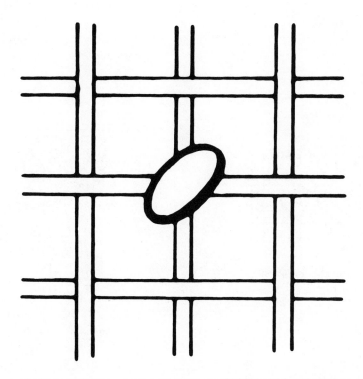

Illustration 2

Basic Needlepoint Stitch

The *tent stitch* (Illustration 2) is the basic needlepoint stitch, slanting from lower left to upper right across the intersections of canvas.

There are three methods of doing the tent stitch: *half cross, continental,* and *basketweave.*

Half Cross

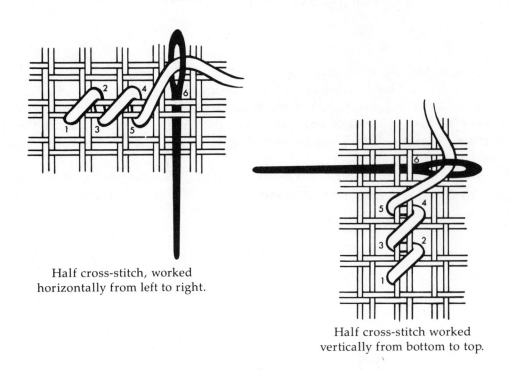

Half cross-stitch, worked
horizontally from left to right.

Half cross-stitch worked
vertically from bottom to top.

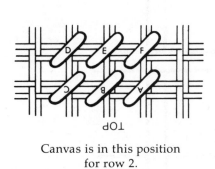

Canvas is in this position
for row 2.

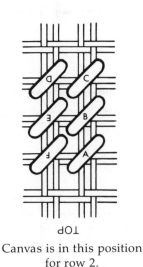

Canvas is in this position
for row 2.

Illustration 3

In half cross (Illustration 3) begin the row at the left-hand side, and work each stitch from lower left across the intersection to upper right. Drop straight down in the back to the next stitch and continue across the row toward the left. To make the second row, turn the canvas upside down and stitch the same way, or, continuing from right to left, reverse the stitch and go from upper right to lower left, across the intersection, then straight up behind the canvas to the upper right again and so on. Half cross should not be worked on mono canvas, as it will slide under the top thread of the woven intersections. Because the back of the stitch goes up and down, it prevents distortion and saves yarn.

Continental

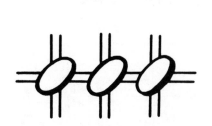

Horizontal tent stitch.

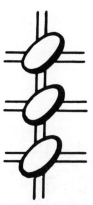

Vertical tent stitch.

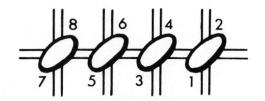

Single row of
horizontal tent stitch.

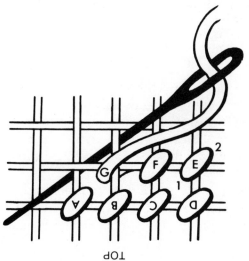

TOP
Canvas is in this position
for Row 2.

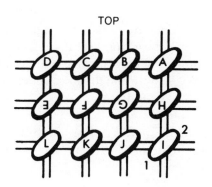

TOP
Canvas is in this position
for Row 3.

Illustration 4

Continental (Illustration 4) looks the same as half cross on the front, but is begun at the right-hand side of the row. Each stitch is made from lower left across the intersection to upper right and on toward the left to the next stitch. The back of each stitch slants and will cause distortion if used in large areas. Continental may be used on all types of canvases but should be restricted to details, outlines, or borders. Continental may also be worked from top to bottom of a row by working down instead of from right to left. The stitch should always go from lower left to upper right, so the canvas must be turned upside down to go on to subsequent rows.

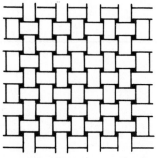

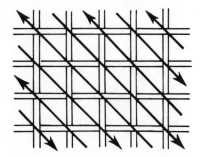

Back of canvas worked
in diagonal tent stitch creates
a "basketweave."

Arrows indicate direction
of diagonal rows.

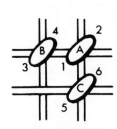

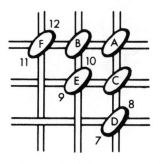

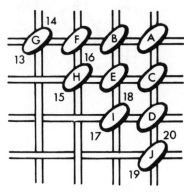

Starting in a corner; B and
C make a descending row
because the vertical canvas
thread is on top.

D, E, and F make an ascending row because the horizontal
canvas thread is on top.

G, H, I, and J make a
descending row.

Illustration 5

Basketweave (Illustration 5) is also stitched across the intersections of canvas from lower left to upper right, but the stitches are worked in diagonal rows from right to left across the area being covered. Because of the sequence, the back of the canvas looks like a woven basket. This takes more yarn, prevents distortion, and is rhythmic and easy to work without having to turn the canvas upside down at every other row. To begin a new row, simply find the intersection of canvas that starts the next diagonal row. Each down row is followed by an up row, and so on.

Stitching two up rows next to each other, or down, will cause a ridge and should be avoided. Up rows are always stitched across canvas intersections that have a horizontal thread on top, and down rows across vertical threads. Remember V/D: *vertical down*. This prevents the yarn from slipping behind the weave of each stitch.

All tent stitching should be begun and ended by burying yarn horizontally or vertically into worked areas, to prevent ridges on the front of the canvas.

In large areas you may want to first outline the section, and then fill it in with basketweave. Do as much basketweave as possible to prevent distortion.

As you count and stitch, try to do the darkest colors last so that dark fibers from worked areas will not be pulled into light areas as they are worked.

Be sure to bury ends of yarn at least one inch, either horizontally or vertically (rather than diagonally), to avoid ridges on the front. If there is not enough worked yarn to bury into, extend a length of yarn two to three inches long to one side (again, horizontally or vertically) and secure it on the front of your work with a temporary or "waste" knot. Later, after you've worked more stitching over the extended yarn length, cut off the knot—carefully! Do the same waste knot when beginning a color in an area that has very little worked yarn. The knot will keep the yarn length taut and enable you to work with both hands.

When working on a frame, you should "push and poke" or "stab" each stitch, using alternate hands, one above and one below the canvas. You should not be able to "sew" or "scoop" each stitch in one motion, because on a frame your piece should be kept very tight.

Mono Canvas Weave

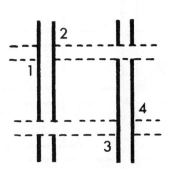

Vertical canvas thread
on top; a descending row.
Out 1, in 2.

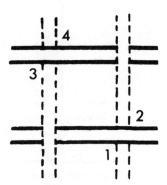

Horizontal canvas thread
on top; an ascending row.
Out 1, in 2.

Illustration 6

When stitching off a frame, scooping is acceptable (certainly faster!), but stabbing always produces a fuller, more even finish. Scooping always distorts more, too.

When stitching basketweave, always alternate "up" and "down" rows—two rows together going in the same direction will produce a diagonal ridge on the front. If using mono canvas, be sure to stitch "down" rows on the intersections that have vertical threads on top, and "up" rows on intersections of threads that have the horizontal threads on top. By *thread*, I refer to woven canvas thread. (*See* Illustration 6).

Try to keep your yarn, canvas, and hands clean, but do not despair if you feel the work is becoming soiled. It can and often *should* be washed when blocked.

Store your project in paper—not plastic! Plastic prevents free circulation of air and can contribute to a flattening and dulling of yarn and even mustiness. Yarn should breathe in order to stay soft and fluffy.

In following the above advice, you will avoid pitfalls and find stitching from *Needlework From Nature* a rich and rewarding experience. By using your own colors and combinations of Christian symbols, you will create a unique expression of your faith in the time-honored technique of needlepoint. Your piece will reflect not only Christian meaning, but also your individual inspiration and devotion.

Counted Cross-Stitch

Counted cross-stitch creates a design with stitches that make Xs on squares woven into fabric. The background is not usually stitched so that the woven fabric provides an attractive contrast to the stitched work. Counted cross-stitch fabrics must be evenly woven so that the charted design will transfer accurately. Evenweave fabrics are available in many counts and colors and may have decorative borders or sectional patterns woven in, but they all share the characteristic of having the same thread count vertically and horizontally.

In my samples I have used linen and Aida cloth, the two most commonly used evenweave fabrics. Linen is woven from flax thread and has great durability and a lovely natural finish. It is available in colors, but is most often seen bleached and unbleached. Although each linen strand is not perfectly even, the weave is, and cross-stitch worked on linen has an unsurpassed traditional quality. Cross-stitches on linen usually are worked across two threads in each direction that form a square (*see* Illustration 7).

Cross-Stitch on Linen

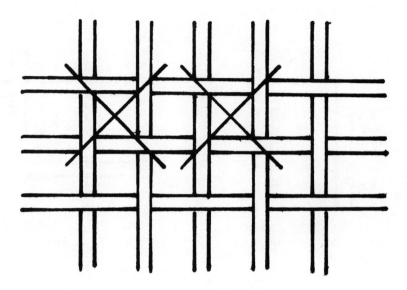

Illustration 7

Linen is available in many counts, most often from 36 to 26, but can be found as fine as 54 threads to the inch. You need not work linen on an embroidery hoop, but if you use one, remove it after every stitching session, to prevent permanent "hoop marks." This rule applies to Aida cloth, too. Depending on the count, one, two, three, or four threads of floss are usually worked on linen.

Aida cloth is a 100 percent cotton fabric woven into squares that are readily perceptible. The X of each stitch is made from corner to corner of each square (*see* Illustration 8).

Aida Cloth Cross-Stitch

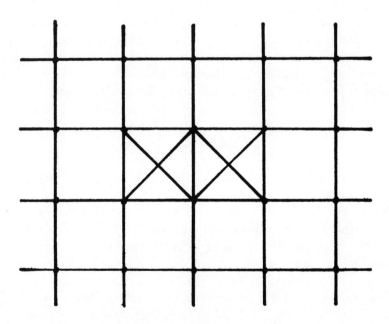

Illustration 8

Aida, available in dozens of colors and in counts from 18 to 11 to the inch, is easy to work and is sold from bolts and in precut packages. Usually a stitcher uses embroidery floss on Aida, but for larger weaves, coton perle number 8 and number 5 may be used. When working with floss, use two, three, four or more strands, depending on the count and the look you are after. Using more strands creates a fuller, plumper, more padded finish. Using fewer strands allows a little fabric to show through each stitch.

Always begin counted work in the middle of the chart and the fabric. Check the finished size before cutting your fabric by using the conversion chart on page 13. Allow one and one-half inches on each side, for finishing. Then fold your fabric in half both ways to locate the middle. Begin stitching at that point.

To stitch, first cut your embroidery floss into a length of fifteen to eighteen inches, separating the threads by holding all six at the top and pulling the number you need straight up from your pinched finger and thumb. This will prevent the threads from twisting as they separate.

Hold a one to one and one-half inch length of thread under the area you're working in and stitch over it—never make knots, except when using waste knots (*see* page 20). Start at the left-hand side of the row and at the lower left of the square and stitch to the upper right. Drop straight down behind to the next lower left corner and repeat across the row as far as that color goes. This is a half cross-stitch. To complete the cross-stitches, come back across the row, stitching from the lower right corner of each square to the upper left.

Cross-Stitch

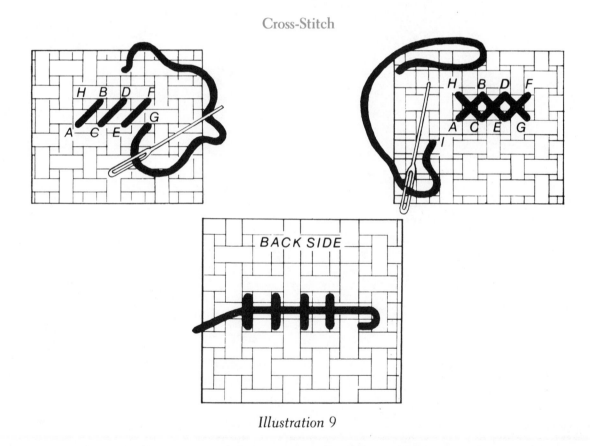

Illustration 9

To end a row, run your thread horizontally or vertically into work already completed. For an even finish, always be sure the stitches on top slant in the same direction throughout your project. On the back of the fabric the floss should always run up and down between stitches—this prevents distortion and saves thread.

For many projects one skein of floss in each color is ample. Projects worked on fabric that takes four or more strands may require many skeins of some colors. Always purchase skeins of one color from the same dye lot. (For information on floss and general stitching guidelines, see pp. 16, 17.)

In general the advice for planning needlepoint projects applies to cross-stitch as well, with the exception that cross-stitch does not wear as well on furniture and so should be used only on surfaces that will not be walked on or knelt on; instead use them for projects that will hang on the wall.

2

ANIMALS

The common appeal, charm, and easy recognizability of animals make them among the most used of Christian symbols. Before the time of Christ, moral stories featuring them instructed man as he observed their behavior with interest and humor, often comparing it to his own. Because of this natural familiarity, today we also find them easy to accept and understand as symbols.

Usually the meaning behind the beast follows directly from its habits (the sheep), its color (the ermine), or its behavior (the lion). Sometimes the symbolic meaning derives from biblical stories (the whale), is connected with the signs or habits of the early Christians (the fish), or is based on popular myth (the dolphin). Some animals may be symbolic of both positive and negative concepts (the griffin), and their meanings may have been influenced by complex and contradictory descriptions in medieval bestiaries. Many are also associated with secular meanings (the rabbit). In any case, their popularity makes them ideal subjects for Christian needlepoint both in the home and church.

Dolphin

The graceful shape of the leaping dolphin appears in artwork of many cultures and has long been associated with friendly intelligence and companionship. The myth that dolphins saved drowning victims by carrying them to safety gave rise in the Christian context to the dolphin as symbol of Christ's triumph over death, His resurrection and salvation, and as Christ Himself. A dolphin with an anchor represents prudence. Shown with an anchor and a boat, the dolphin symbolizes the Church and the Christian soul guided by Christ. The dolphin with a trident represents the Crucifixion.

Ermine

The ermine's white coat has naturally led to its Christian association with chastity and purity.

Fish

In Christian symbolism, the fish represents Christ, Christ the Savior, the Eucharist, the Passion, Baptism, and believers. The Greek word for fish was used by early Christians as an esoteric sign of their faith because its letters (*icthyus*) were also the initials of the Greek phrase "Jesus Christ, Son of God, Savior." Fish shown with loaves symbolize Holy Communion, and three fish together represent the Holy Trinity.

Griffin

The griffin, a mythical beast with the body of a lion, the head and wings of an eagle, and the tail of a serpent, usually symbolizes Christ, but can also mean those who oppress and persecute Christians—the antichrists.

Lamb

The lamb represents Christ, Savior and Redeemer, and the Passion. When shown with Christ, the lamb symbolizes the sinner rescued by Him. The traditional sacrificial lamb of Passover associates the lamb with Easter and Christ's sacrifice. Also it may symbolize the virtues of temperance, prudence, charity, meekness, patience, and docility. Four lambs symbolize the Apostles. A lamb holding a staff with a banner at the top, decorated with a cross, represents the Resurrection and Christ's victory over death. When a lamb is shown sitting on a book sealed with seven seals, it symbolizes the lamb of the apocalypse.

Sheep in a flock may represent the Church, the Apostles, or a congregation.

Lion

King of the beasts in secular symbolism, the Christian lion represents Christ as king of all the people, as well as the attributes of strength, majesty, courage, resolution, unceasing mercy, fortitude, fidelity in love, and protective vigilance. The lion can also symbolize the Resurrection. A winged lion represents Saint Mark, and Daniel is associated with the lion. The lion may also depict fierceness, pride, and rarely, evil or Satan.

Rabbit or Hare

Long recognized as a secular symbol of fertility, the rabbit or hare is known to the Christian as a symbol of Christ's Passion and may also represent the faithful. A white rabbit at Mary's feet symbolizes the Virgin's conquest over lust.

Whale

The primary symbolic meanings of the whale —the resurrection and salvation of the faithful— derives from its role in the story of Jonah. Although today we view the harmless whale as beautiful and fascinating, to the early Christians the whale's vastness, mystery, and huge mouth made it a frightening presence. Hence the whale may also represent the devil and his cunning, hell, containment, and concealment.

BEFORE YOU START STITCHING, be sure your fabric or canvas is big enough. Use the stitch conversion chart on page 13 to find out how big the design will be on your material; then find the middle and start counting from the middle of the chart. Remember each symbol represents one stitch. Count, and count carefully!

Above all, enjoy the fascinating process of seeing the design emerge, stitch by stitch, from your blank surface.

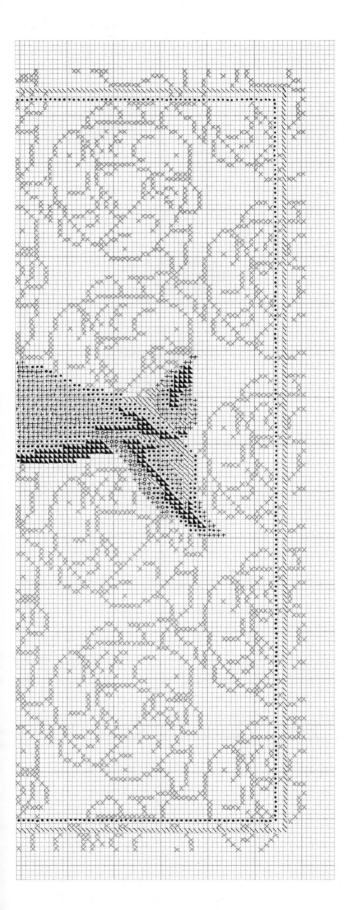

Dolphin and
Three-Fish Background

STITCH COUNTS

Horizontal/Vertical   211 x 165

KEY – BLACK SYMBOLS	PATERNYAN #
◣ CHARCOAL GREY – DARK	200
• CHARCOAL GREY – MEDIUM	201
+ CHARCOAL GREY – LIGHT	202
\ GREY	203
○ GREY – VERY LIGHT	204

GREEN SYMBOL	DMC PERLE
X LIGHT SEAFOAM GREEN	993

BACKGROUND	PATERN YAN #
DARK SEAFOAM GREEN	595

Ermine and Fir

STITCH COUNTS

Horizontal/Vertical   191 x 184

SYMBOL	COLOR	PATERNAYAN #
◣	BLACK	220
·	OFF WHITE	261
L	RUST	721
■	V. DARK GREEN	660
S	DARK GREEN	661
X	MED. GREEN	662
O	LIGHT GREEN	664
•	DARK LIME	670
\	LIGHT LIME	672
✳	BROWN	740
+	GOLDEN BROWN	742
↑	YELLOW-BROWN	744
△	LIGHT GREY	212
—	DARK GREY	211

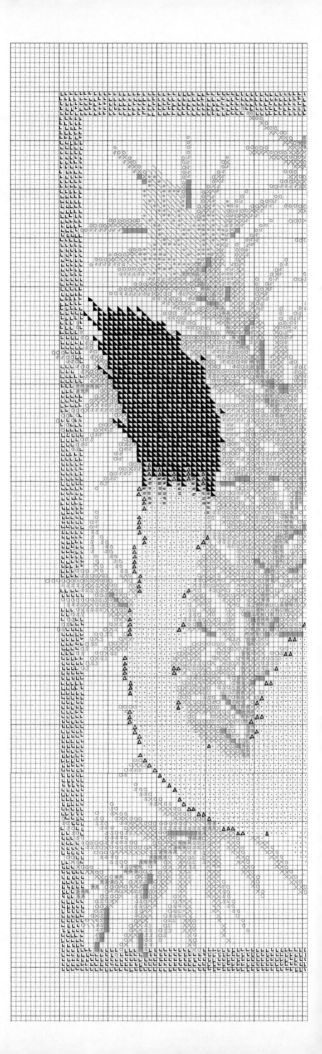

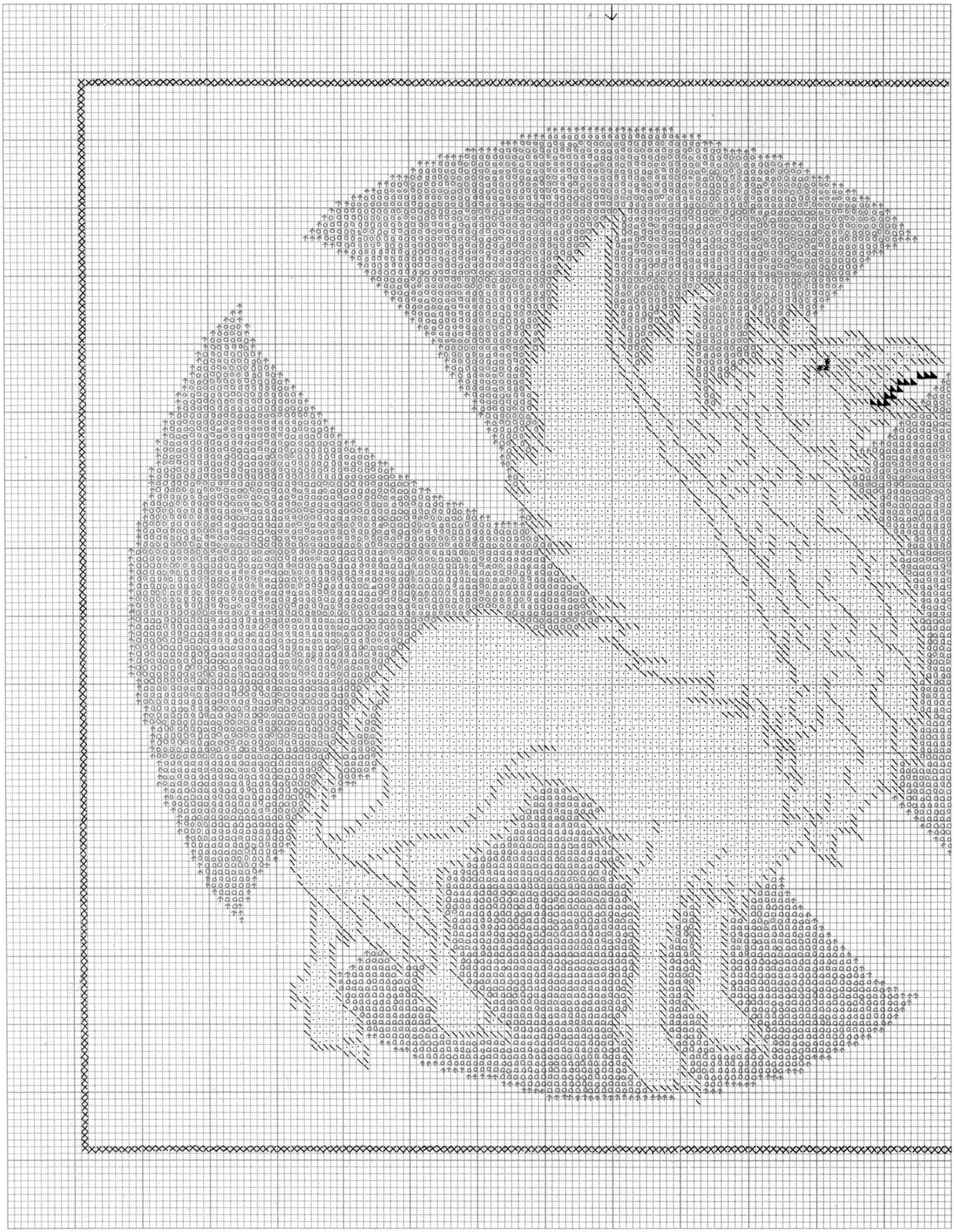

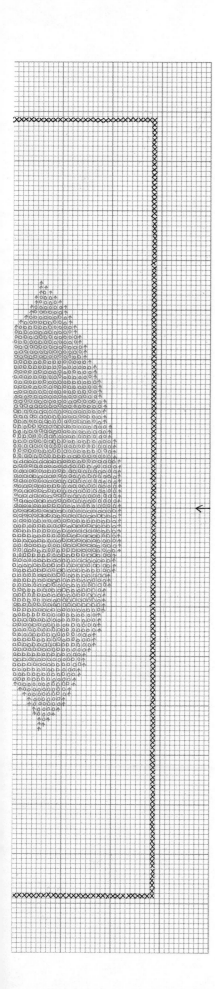

Griffin and Cross Formée

STITCH COUNTS

Horizontal/Vertical   180 x 180

SYMBOL	COLOR	DMC FLOSS #
×	NILE GREEN	913
\	GREY	926
.	WHITE	BLANC — WITH ONE STRAND SILVER FILAMENT
O	TANGERINE — LIGHT	742
↑	ORANGE SPICE — MEDIUM	721
✳	CANARY — BRIGHT	973
◤	RED	349

Lamb and Grain

STITCH COUNTS

Horizontal/Vertical   156 x 156

SYMBOL	COLOR	DMC #
X	BLUE – MEDIUM	796
		MEDICI #
◣	BLACK	BLACK
.	WHITE	BLANC
*	HAZELNUT BROWN	323
↑	OLD GOLD	525
o	GOLDEN YELLOW – LIGHT	T748
\	GREY	T380
•	AVOCADO GREEN – MEDIUM	402
s	AVOCADO GREEN – LIGHT	420
BACKGROUND	BLUE – LIGHT	T199

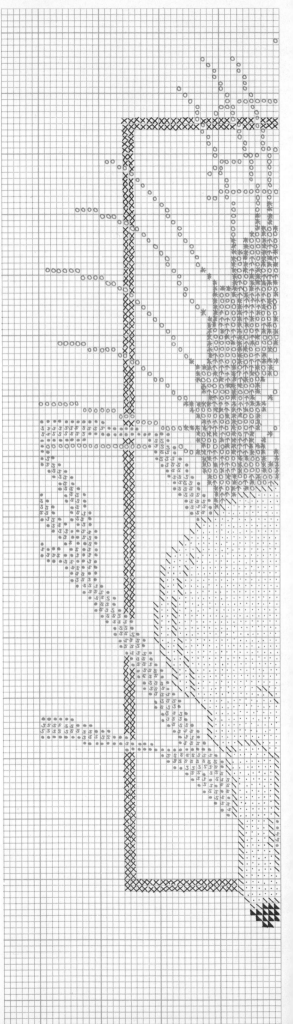

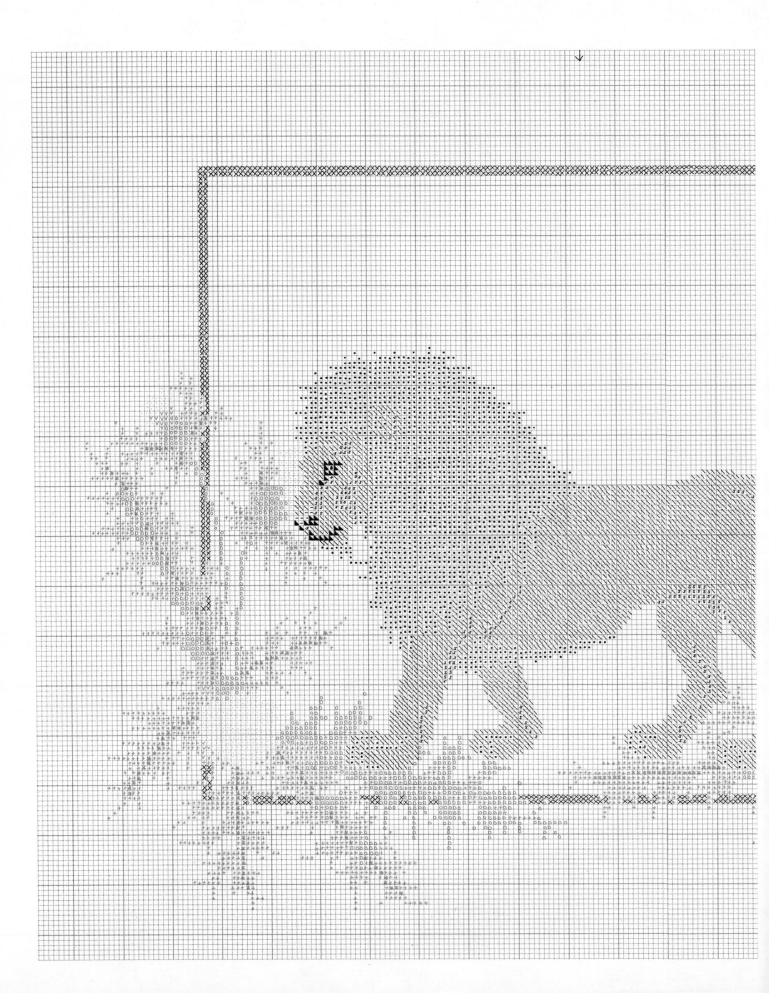

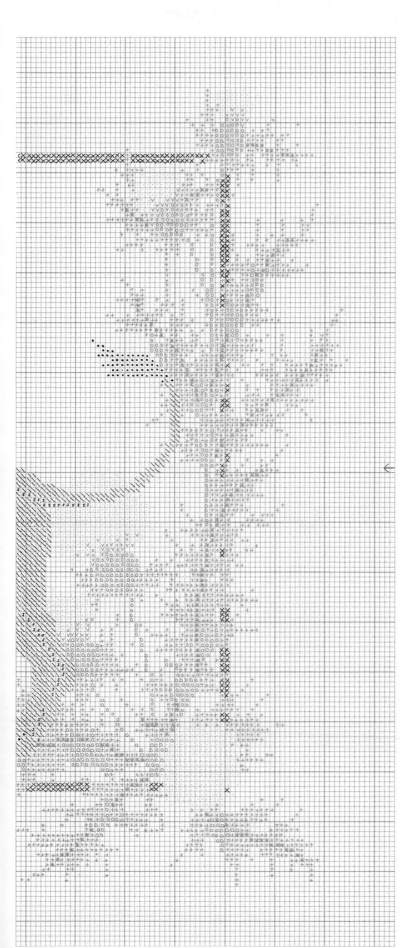

Lion and Thistle

STITCH COUNTS

Horizontal/Vertical 206 x 179

SYMBOL	COLOR	DMC#
BACKGROUND	CREAM	746
X	VIOLET — VERY DARK	550
◤	BLACK	310
⁕	WHITE	BLANC
		PATERNAYAN PERSIAN#
−	OLD GOLD — VERY LIGHT	774
⁂	GREEN — DARK	691
+	GREEN — MEDIUM	693
o	GREEN — LIGHT	694
v	PURPLE	311
·	PURPLE — LIGHT	313
•	COFFEE BROWN — DARK	422
ʃ	HAZELNUT BROWN	441
\	TAN — VERY LIGHT	443

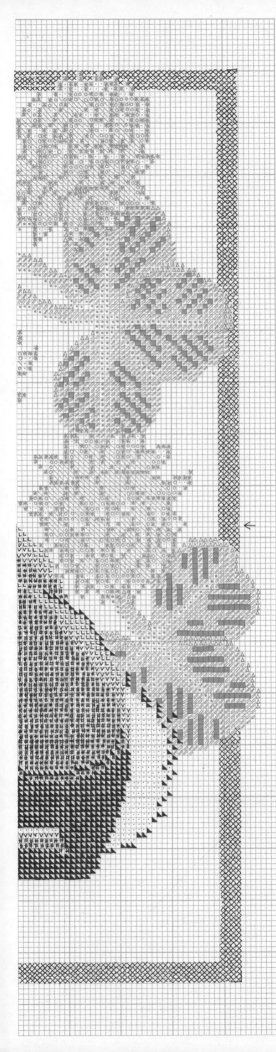

Rabbit and Clover

STITCH COUNTS

Horizontal/Vertical   182 x 185

SYMBOL	COLOR	PATERNAYAN PERSIAN #
✳	PURPLE – DARK	310
＼	PURPLE – MEDIUM	312
O	PURPLE – LIGHT	314
•	GREEN – DARK	600
//	GREEN – MEDIUM	603
Δ	GREEN – LIGHT	326
·	WHITE	261
◣	BROWN – DARK	461
＃	MOCHA BROWN – DARK	463
V	MOCHA BROWN – MEDIUM	464
L	MOCHA BROWN – LIGHT	465
■	GARNET – VERY DARK	920
×	CRANBERRY – DARK	930
+	PINK	326

Trout and Water

STITCH COUNTS

Horizontal/Vertical   177 x 177

SYMBOL	COLOR	PATERNAYAN #
\	DARK BLUE	552
BACKGROUND	MED. BLUE	553
+	LIGHT BLUE	554
◣	V. DARK GREY	221
×	MED. GREY	234
0	LIGHT GREY	236
·	OFF WHITE	261
⋀	GREEN-GOLD	753
●	DARK PINK	904
3	MED. PINK	906
L	LIGHT PINK	964

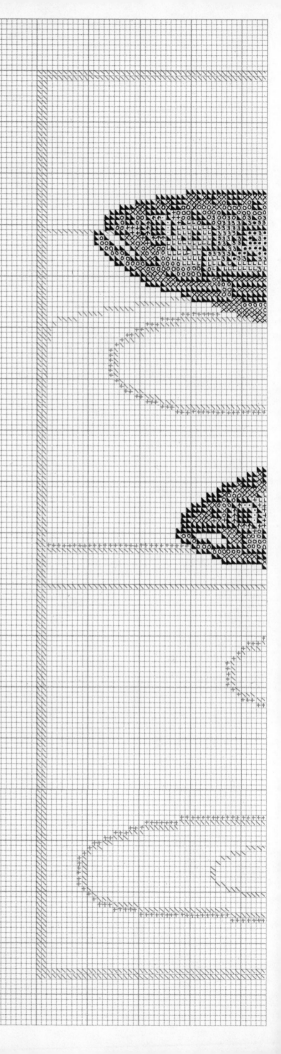

Whale, Scallop Shell, and Water

STITCH COUNTS

Horizontal/Vertical 214 x 165

SYMBOL	COLOR	PATERNAYAN	DMC PERLE	1 STRAND DMC FLOSS
×	DARK GREEN	520		500
BACKGROUND	LIGHT GREEN	525		504
■	DARK GREEN		501	
↑	LIGHT GREEN		504	
3	WHITE		WHITE	
◣	DARK PEWTER GREY	210		
•	PEWTER GREY	211		
/	LIGHT PEWTER GREY	212		
o	PEARL GREY	213		
·	LIGHT PEARL GREY	246		
*	DARK COPPER	400		
+	COPPER	403		
\	LIGHT COPPER	405		
L	OFF WHITE	261		
S	DARK GOLD	734		
-	LIGHT GOLD	704		

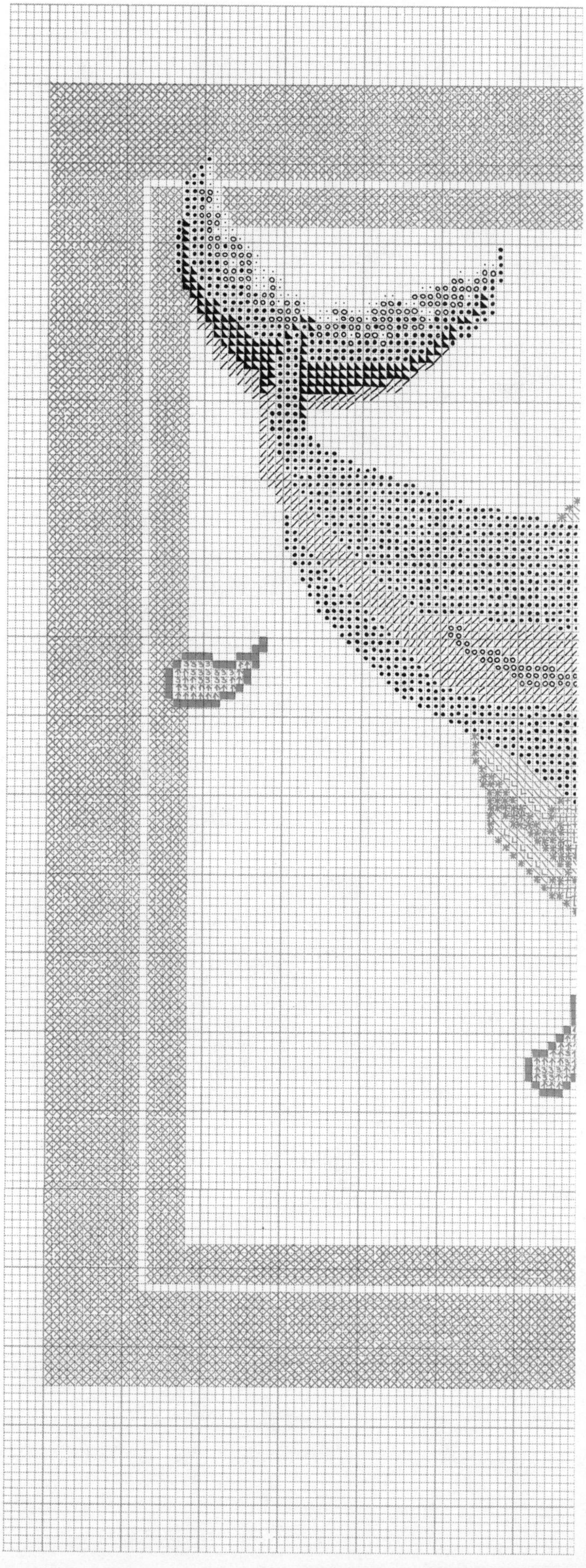

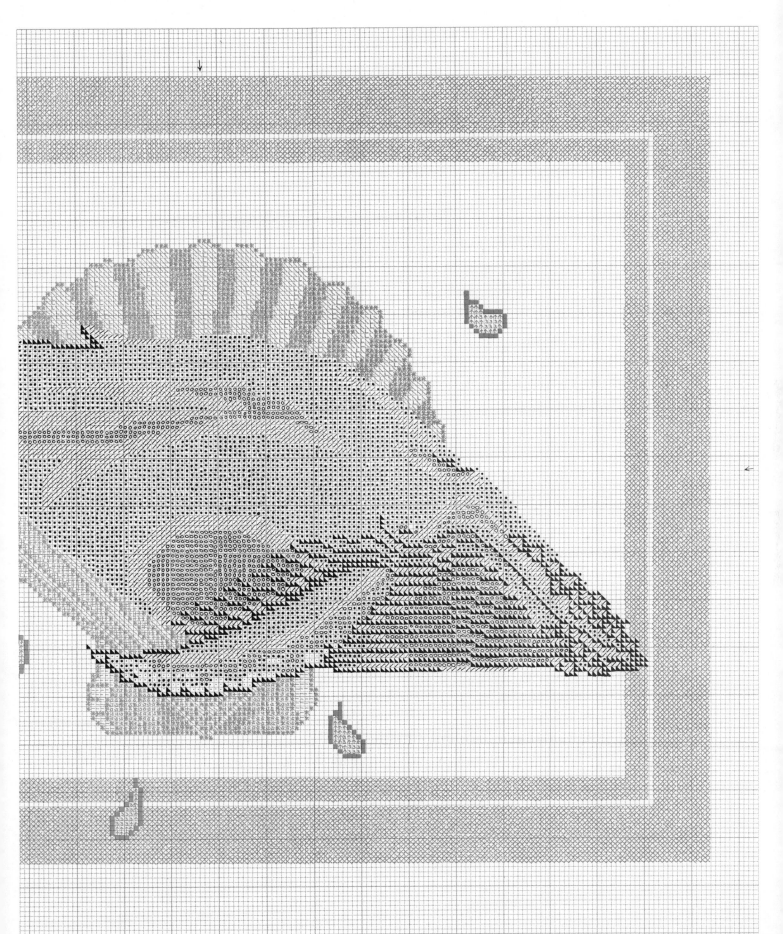

3
BIRDS AND INSECTS

Birds and insects represent the most opposite concepts within any one category of Christian symbols from nature. Their abundant variety in behavior and appearance may explain their often antithetical meanings. From soaring to plunging (the eagle) ; from proud display (the peacock), to shy camouflage (the sparrow); from fabulous myth (the phoenix), to everyday reality (the dove), birds and insects present conflicting images that excite our spirits and imagination. We may fear them, admire their freewheeling flight, or keep them as pets. In any case, they remain spirit stirring and have been understood symbolically in art and crafts from ancient times. In needlework birds and insects may be depicted in their natural settings and attitudes or in stylized shapes, depending upon the familiarity of the symbol. The dove is universally understood in its most simplified outline, whereas the heron is more readily recognized when shown in its habitat.

Most of the birds that convey Christian concepts are mentioned in the Bible. Some emerged in medieval bestiaries and were adopted by Christians. Others transfigure ancient secular symbols. All the following birds and insects convey Christian concepts, but can be appreciated, too, as decorative designs for pillows, piano benches, bellpulls, wall hangings, kneelers, or runners, in the home or the church.

Bee

Throughout civilization the bee's hard work and orderliness have impressed people of many cultures. In Christian symbolism the bee figures as the representative of industry, busy forethought, creativity, activity, diligence, and good order. The bee's production of honey has also led to its being symbolic of sweetness, religious eloquence, and the virginity of Mary. Its ceaseless activity also makes the bee a symbol of Christian zealousness and unremitting effort to become virtuous. (*See* Lily design.)

Butterfly

Referred to in Greek as *psyche*, the butterfly is recognized by many sources as referring to the Christian soul. Because of its lowly origins as a caterpillar and its evolution through the drab stage of chrysalis to the magnificent winged insect, the butterfly also symbolizes metamorphosis and more specifically the life, death, and resurrection of man as well as Christ. It can also symbolize Christian love and the promise of eternal life.

Cock

The cock symbolizes watchfulness and vigilance. Christ's prediction that his disciple would deny him three times before the cock crowed also links it with Saint Peter. The cock's association with Saint Peter also makes it a symbol of repentance and of the Passion.

Crane

In Christian artwork the crane is often depicted observing a scene of significance. In this role, it symbolizes vigilance and loyalty. Legends about its behavior have led to the crane's association with a good life and works and monastic good order.

Dove

The dove, one of the most widely depicted of Christian symbols, has many meanings in addition to the universally familiar one of peace. When shown with an olive branch, the dove signifies peace, but is also associated with Noah and the ark and signifies divine forgiveness, God's reconciliation with man, and hope.

The dove may also signify divine inspiration. Its presence represents that of the Holy Spirit, and it appears in scenes of the creation, the Annunciation, and Christ's Baptism.

When the dove is shown with wings outspread, shedding rays of light, it represents the Holy Ghost.

Doves may depict souls, especially redeemed souls. A single dove issuing from a body indicates the soul departing at death. A dove shown drinking from a fountain or pecking at bread symbolizes the soul nourished by the Eucharist.

Seven doves represent the seven gifts of the Holy Ghost; twelve doves, the twelve Apostles. A flock of doves represents the Church.

The dove's appearance and demeanor have led to its being symbolic of gentleness, guilelessness, innocence, faithfulness, simplicity, gentle affection, and especially purity.

Eagle

When shown with a halo, the eagle symbolizes Saint John. It is often incorporated into the carving of the lectern from which the gospel is read and may in that context represent the inspiration of the gospels. The eagle's ability to soar and its legendary ability to renew itself by flying close to the sun, searing its feathers, and then plunging into water have led to its association with the Resurrection, the Ascen-

sion, Baptism, and the attainment of grace. The eagle may also simply depict the soaring spirit. In general this magnificent bird symbolizes courage, faith, and contemplation. Thought to always leave a portion of its prey to those that follow, it also symbolizes generosity.

As a soaring and plunging bird of prey, the eagle sometimes represents the negative attributes of pride and worldly power or ravishment of the soul.

Heron

The heron represents the souls of the elect in Christian symbolism.

Peacock

Legend held that the flesh of the peacock did not decay, which led to the Christian interpretation of the peacock as a symbol of immortality. In addition, because the plumage of its tail renews itself every year, the peacock represents the Resurrection. The eyes of the peacock's tail feathers are symbolic of the all-seeing eyes of the Church.

Contrarily, the peacock's strutting display may represent worldly pride and vanity.

Phoenix

The mythical phoenix, a bird with the body of an eagle and the head of a pheasant, was reputed to burn itself on a funeral pyre every three to five hundred years, then to rise from its own ashes three days later. This triumph over death naturally appeared symbolic to early Christians, who saw in the legendary bird an incarnation of the resurrection of the dead and the hope of eternal life. Later the phoenix was seen as a symbol of Christ's triumph over death, and it now signifies the Crucifixion and Resurrection.

The phoenix may also represent faith and constancy.

Sparrow

The sparrow symbolizes God's protection of the lowliest.

Stork

The stork's annual migration north announces the coming of spring. In Christian symbolism, this has led to the stork's association with the Annunciation and the Advent of Christ. Perhaps it also explains the familiar myth that storks bring babies.

Its monogamy and good parenting habits have led to the stork's symbolic role as emblem of vigilance, filial piety, prudence, and faithfulness.

In addition the stork's white feathers associate it with chastity.

Swallow

Legend describes the swallow as burrowing in the mud to hibernate in winter. Its legendary reemergence in spring associates the swallow with the Resurrection. In scenes of the Nativity or the Annunciation, the nestling swallow symbolizes the Incarnation of Christ.

BEFORE YOU START STITCHING, be sure your fabric or canvas is big enough. Use the stitch conversion chart on page 13 to find out how big the design will be on your material; then find the middle and start counting from the middle of the chart. Remember each symbol represents one stitch. Count, and count carefully!

Above all, enjoy the fascinating process of seeing the design emerge, stitch by stitch, from your blank surface.

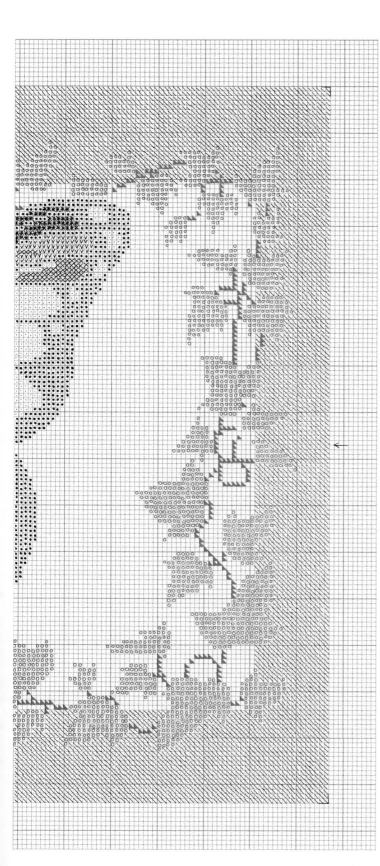

Butterfly and Ivy

STITCH COUNTS

Horizontal/Vertical   227 x 154

Symbol	Color	Paternayan #
◤	LIME GREEN - DK	670
O	LIME GREEN	672
BACKGROUND	DARK RED	840
\	BLUE	501
•	DARK BROWN	114
*	DARK RUST	720
V	RUST	722
×	ORANGE/BROWN	724
.	YELLOW	727

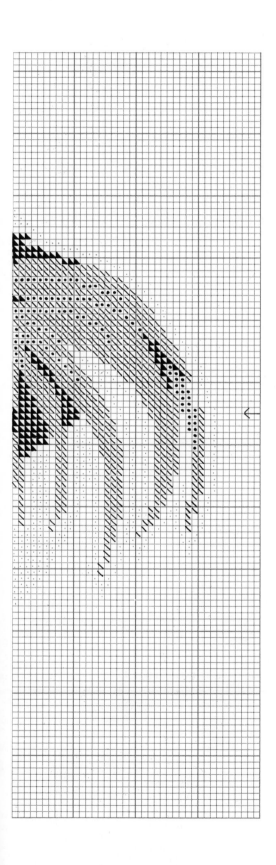

Cock

STITCH COUNTS

Horizontal/Vertical   150 x 150

SYMBOL	COLOR	DMC #
BACKGROUND	WHITE	BLANC
◣	BLACK	310
×	STEEL GREY – DARK	414
●	PISTACHIO GREEN – ULTRA DARK	890
\	EMERALD GREEN – VERY DARK	909
↑	EMERALD GREEN – LIGHT	912
S	CHRISTMAS GOLD	783
·	LEMON – DARK	444
o	TOPAZ – LIGHT	726
—	BEIGE BROWN – DARK	839
V	TERRA COTTA – DARK	355
#	COPPER	921
I	MAHOGANY – VERY LIGHT	402
+	DRAB BROWN – DARK	611
L	BEIGE GREY – DARK	642
✱	GARNET – MEDIUM	815
//	CORAL – DARK	349

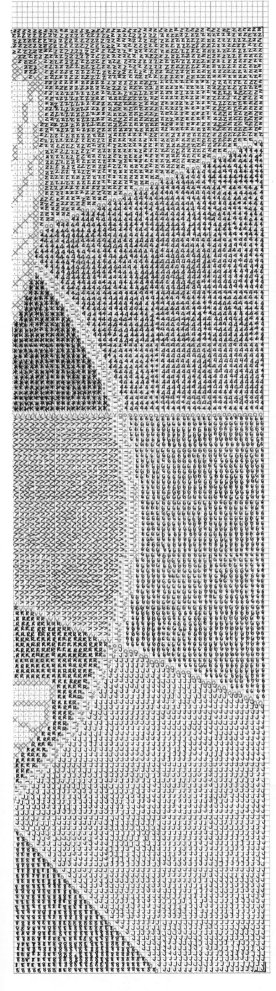

Dove and Aureole

STITCH COUNTS

Horizontal/Vertical   180 x 180

	SYMBOL	COLOR	PATERNAYAN PERSIAN #	DMC COTON PERLE #
DOVE & RAYS	▲	BLACK	220	
	·	WHITE	260	
	X	GREY	212	
	O	LEMON – LIGHT		445
	V	LEMON – DARK		444
	•	CHRISTMAS GOLD		783
	S	TOPAZ		725
	–	TOPAZ – VERY LIGHT		727
OUTER COLORS	↑	GOLDEN YELLOW – V. LIGHT	704	
	3	ORANGE SPICE – LIGHT	803	
	C	APRICOT	854	
	\	GERANIUM	954	
	Δ	SALMON	952	
	I	MAUVE – MEDIUM	913	
	E	VIOLET – LIGHT	323	
	Z	LAVENDER – DARK	313	
	4	PURPLE – LIGHT	333	
	6	BLUE VIOLET – MEDIUM	343	
	J	DELFT – MEDIUM	544	
	8	PEACOCK BLUE – LIGHT	584	
	K	SEAGREEN	577	
	T	PINE GREEN – LIGHT	623	
	7	AVOCADO GREEN – V. LIGHT	673	
	Y	AVOCADO GREEN – ULTRA LIGHT	763	
INNER COLORS	∴	CANARY – BRIGHT	772	
	/	CANARY – DEEP	770	
	2	TANGERINE	800	
	L	BURNT ORANGE – DARK	852	
	N	CORAL RED – VERY DARK	969	
	5	CHRISTMAS RED – DARK	940	
	W	GARNET – V. DARK	901	
	9	MAUVE – DARK	910	
	*	VIOLET – VERY DARK	311	
	>	PURPLE	331	
	R	BLUE VIOLET – DARK	340	
	∩	DELFT	542	
	D	PEACOCK BLUE – DARK	581	
	F	AQUAMARINE	574	
	Y	CHRISTMAS GREEN	632	
	#	PARROT GREEN	671	

Eagle and Columbine

STITCH COUNTS

Horizontal/Vertical   198 x 252

SYMBOL	COLOR	MEDICI #
+	BEAVER GREY — MEDIUM	204
−	BEAVER GREY — LIGHT	204A
◣	BLACK	NOIR
·	WHITE	BLANC
●	COFFEE BROWN — DARK	306
✳	BROWN — MEDIUM	300
O	BROWN — LIGHT	301
\	TAN	302
#	PINK	7102
×	GREEN — DARK	415
↑	GREEN — MEDIUM	406
S	GREEN — LIGHT	7369
V	CORNFLOWER BLUE — DARK	7899
L	CORNFLOWER BLUE — LIGHT	7798
//	CHRISTMAS GOLD	7484
I	TOPAZ — VERY LIGHT	7026

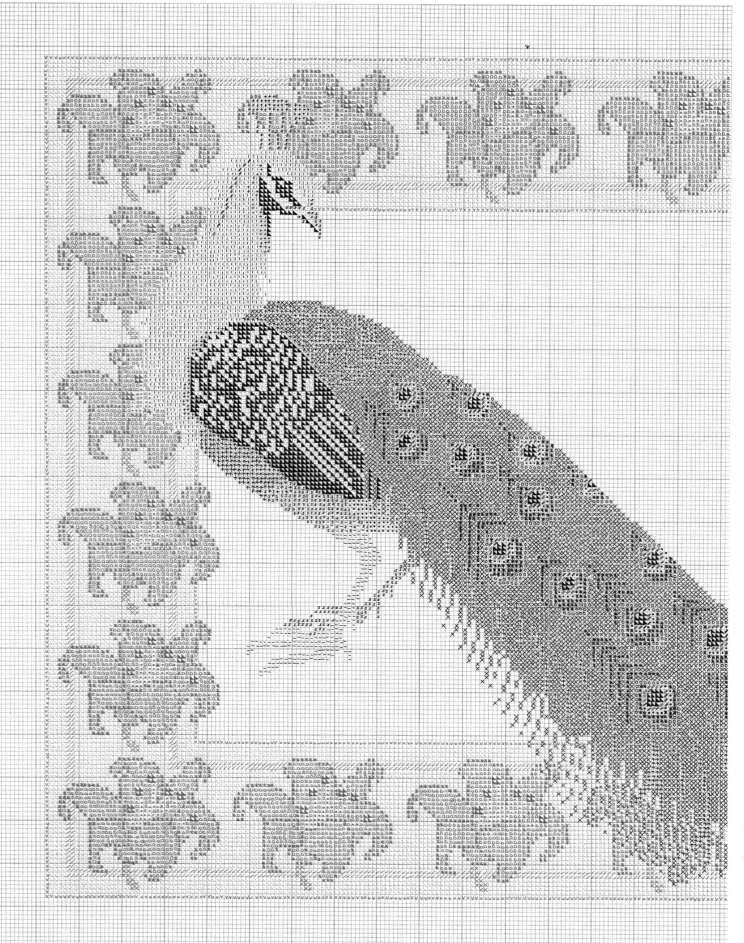

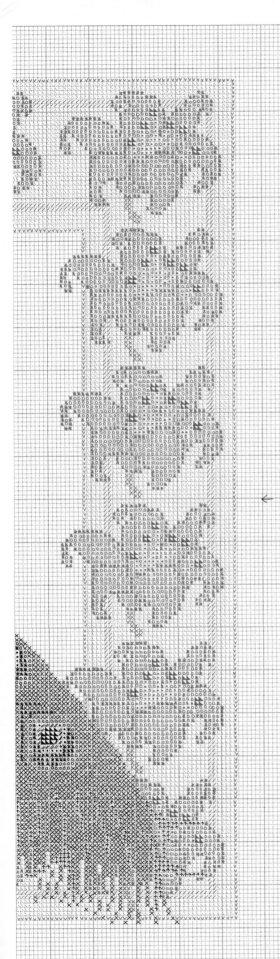

Peacock and Lilies

STITCH COUNTS

Horizontal/Vertical   216 x 200

SYMBOL	COLOR	MEDICI #
··	OFF WHITE	BLANC
BACKGROUND	CHRISTMAS GOLD	303A
v	WEDGEWOOD — LIGHT	7997
/	WEDGEWOOD — DARK	7993
		DMC #
◤	BLACK	310
·	WHITE	BLANC
⌃	CHRISTMAS GREEN	699
X	EMERALD GREEN — MED.	911
✳	TOPAZ — MEDIUM	783
●	COPPER — MEDIUM	920
+	BLUE — VERY DARK	824
I	ELECTRIC BLUE — DARK	995
//	ELECTRIC BLUE — MED.	996
S	STEEL GREY — DARK	414
—	PEARL GREY	415

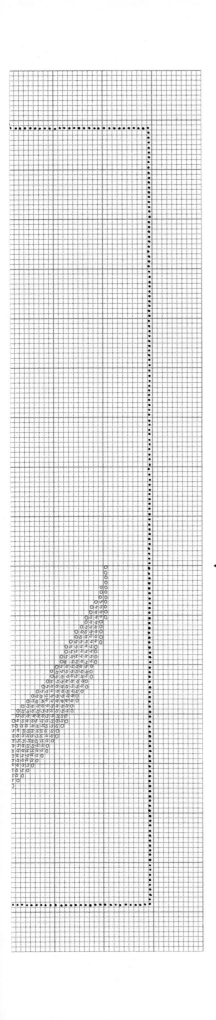

←

Phoenix and Flames

STITCH COUNTS

Horizontal/Vertical   180 x 180

SYMBOL	COLOR	DMC #
\	GREY	926
.	WHITE	BLANC — WITH 1 STRAND SILVER FILAMENT
×	RED	349
↑	ORANGE SPICE – MEDIUM	721
o	TANGERINE – LIGHT	742
S	YELLOW – MEDIUM	743
✳	CANARY – BRIGHT	973
V	TOPAZ – VERY LIGHT	727
◣	JADE – VERY LIGHT	564
+	GOLDEN YELLOW – VERY LIGHT	3078
•	NILE GREEN	913

Sparrow and Triparted Cross

STITCH COUNTS

Horizontal/Vertical   171 x 171

SYMBOL	COLOR	DMC PERLE #
.	WHITE	BLANC
o	SPORTSMAN FLESH	945
s	SPORTSMAN FLESH – DARK	407
x	COPPER	632
+	BEIGE BROWN – V. DARK	838
•	BLACK BROWN	3371
↑	TOPAZ – V. LIGHT	727
\	OLD GOLD – MED	729
I	OLD GOLD – V. LIGHT	677
◣	BLACK	310
E	BEIGE GREY – V. DARK	640
–	BEIGE GREY – MEDIUM	644
✳	PISTACHIO GREEN – MED	7369 – MEDICI
/	PISTACHIO GREEN – LIGHT	7871 – MEDICI
∴	PEACH	505A – MEDICI

Swallow and Cross Masculy

STITCH COUNTS

Horizontal/Vertical   171 x 171

SYMBOL	COLOR	MEDICI #
✳	GREY – MEDIUM	508
\	GREY – LIGHT	509
.	PEACH – LIGHT	504A
		DMC #
◣	BLACK	310
×	PEWTER GREY – DARK	413
o	PEARL GREY – V. LIGHT	762
•	NAVY BLUE – MEDIUM	311
+	NAVY BLUE – LIGHT	312
∴	BABY BLUE – MEDIUM	334
﹂	DRAB BROWN – V. DARK	610
–	DRAB BROWN – DARK	611
V	MAHOGANY – DARK	400
I	COPPER – LIGHT	922
/	MAHOGANY – VERY LIGHT	402
＃	WHITE	BLANC

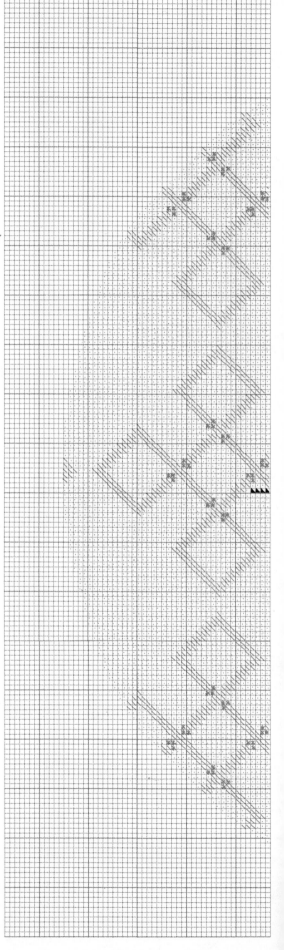

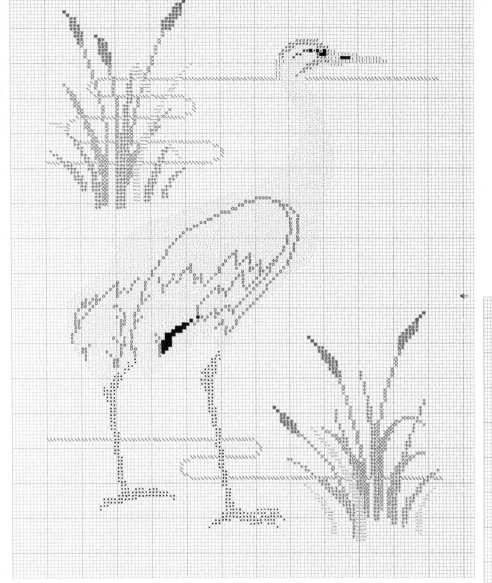

Crane

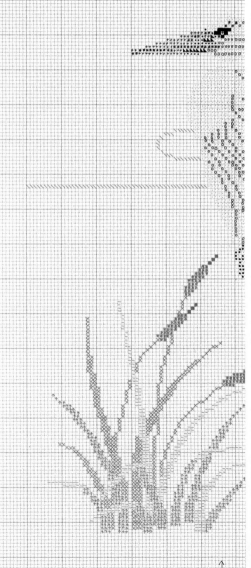

Heron

Trout and water

Phoenix and flames

Griffin and cross formée

Grapes

Olive and Latin cross

Eagle and columbine

Sparrow and triparted cross

Dove and aureole

Peacock and lilies

Iris

Crane, heron, and stork

Ermine and fir

Lamb and grain

Lion and thistle

Dolphin and three-fish background

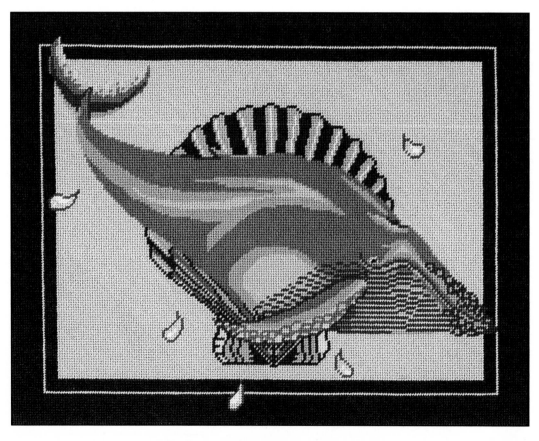

Whale, scallop shell, and water

CRANE
STITCH COUNTS

Horizontal/Vertical 113 x 173

SYMBOL	COLOR	MEDICI #
X	DARK GREEN	417
↑	MEDIUM GREEN	418
−	LIGHT GREEN	419
\	BLUE	208
·	WHITE	BLANC
+	LIGHT GOLD	326
■	BLACK	BLACK
*	BROWN	306
o	LIGHT GREY	509
●	V. DARK GREY	506
l	PEACH	504A
ſ	DARK RED	126
#	MEDIUM GREY	508

HERON
STITCH COUNTS

Horizontal/Vertical 188 x 113

SYMBOL	COLOR	MEDICI #
X	DARK GREEN	417
↑	MEDIUM GREEN	418
−	LIGHT GREEN	419
\	BLUE	208
·	WHITE	BLANC
+	LIGHT GOLD	326
■	BLACK	BLACK
*	BROWN	306
o	LIGHT GREY	509
●	V. DARK GREY	506
◣	GOLD	303
#	MEDIUM GREY	508

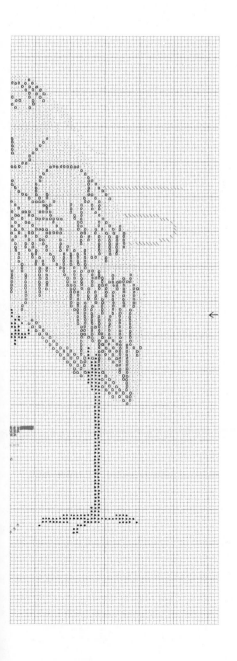

Stork

STITCH COUNTS

Horizontal/Vertical   113 x 160

SYMBOL	COLOR	MEDICI #
×	DARK GREEN	417
↑	MEDIUM GREEN	418
–	LIGHT GREEN	419
\	BLUE	208
·	WHITE	BLANC
■	BLACK	BLACK
✳	BROWN	306
o	LIGHT GREY	509
✳	MEDIUM GREY	508
◣	DARK GREY	507
•	V. DARK GREY	506
ς	RED/ORANGE	127
ı	TANGERINE	129

4

PLANTS

The annual cycles of plants have impressed and fascinated us from the beginning of time. Seasonally dying and renewing, plants have profound psychological and spiritual significance, saddening or cheering us, reminding us of the passage of time, the inevitability of death, the promise of renewal. We depend on plants and flowers for physical and aesthetic nourishment, planting and nurturing them, gathering them, arranging them, gazing at them with love and wonder. Naturally then, plants have assumed a symbolic role throughout the ages in art and decoration.

For the Christian, the depiction of plants and flowers intrinsically expresses the beauty of creation, the power and mystery of the divine, the love of God for His people. In the millefleurs tapestries of the fifteenth century, multitudes of plants and flowers proliferate across the backgrounds, expressing the anonymous weavers' love of nature and of God. To the medieval artisan, plants were a natural and familiar expression of devotion. Over seventy species have been since identified in the tapestries of the *Hunt of the Unicorn,* many of which have specific Christian meaning and are used today to express the same concepts—for example, the lily, iris, and columbine.

Some plants and flowers used in contemporary art and decoration came to us from the Bible, figuring there in stories, lessons, and observations. The bulrush is mentioned four times in the Bible, most memorably in the story of Moses, and hence is imbued with Christian symbolism.

In needlework, plants may be represented realistically or stylistically. Repeated stylized motifs make excellent backgrounds, borders, or overall patterns for chair seats, kneelers, wall hangings, or cushions. On the other hand, a single realistic bloom or spray or bouquet can be eloquently expressive in the church or in the home. The designs that follow may be used singly, combined, or repeated to depict Christian devotion through the natural beauty of plants and flowers.

Bulrush

The familiar and lowly bulrush represents humility and faithfulness. Its role in the story of Moses associates the bulrush with the source of salvation.

Clover

Clover has antipathetic meanings in Christian symbolism, depending on the number of leaves depicted. The three-leafed clover, a natural tre-

foil, represents the Trinity. Goodness and "good luck" are symbolized by the four-leafed clover, but the clover shown with five leaves denotes harm and "bad luck."

Columbine

The dovelike shape and color of the columbine's flower was the source of its name—the Latin word *columba* means "dove." The columbine shares the dove's symbolic meaning of the Holy Ghost. When shown with seven blossoms, the columbine represents the seven sorrows of Mary. The flower may also simply depict sorrow. (*See* Eagle Background.)

Fir

With its myriad evergreen needles, the fir represents the patient and the heavenly elect.

Grain

Grain, wheat, or corn symbolizes the host, Christ's body or flesh. When shown in scenes of the nativity or adoration, sheaves of wheat represent Christ as Savior or Christ's mission as Savior of mankind. When combined with bunches of grapes, grain refers to the bread of the Eucharist, and grapes refer to the wine. (*See* Backgrounds.)

Grape, Grape Leaf, Grape Vine

The grape, its leaf and vine are among the most ancient of Christian symbols and are referred to metaphorically throughout the Bible. Jesus as Savior was called the true vine and may be symbolized by the grape leaf and vine. Grapes allude to wine and may therefore symbolize the Passion, the Crucifixion, and Jesus' blood. Grapes also represent the Eucharist and when combined with ears of wheat or grain specifically denote the wine and bread of Holy Communion. The grape harvest may symbolize the Resurrection.

Iris

The iris, or sword lily, represents Mary, the Immaculate Conception, and Mary's piercing sorrow during the Passion and Crucifixion. The attributes associated with Mary may also be depicted by the iris—beauty, humility, sweetness, uprightness, virginity. As it is considered one of the flowers that blooms there, the iris may refer to paradise.

Ivy

The clinging ivy symbolizes attachment, undying affection, and fidelity. Because it stays green all year, the vine is also associated with eternal life. It may also symbolize death and immortality.

Lily

Originally a symbol of purity, the lily later became associated with Mary, her purity, chastity, and virginity. A lily among thorns represents the Immaculate Conception. Lilies are often present in scenes of the Annunciation and have become associated with the archangel Gabriel as well as Mary.

Olive Branch or Tree

The olive tree's fruitfulness, its rich yield of oil, the shade it provides, and its ubiquitousness have made it a symbol of plenty, peace, harmony, and healing. Its abundance is emblematic of God's providence, good will, and generosity to His people. Because the dove returned to Noah with an olive sprig, together bud and branch symbolize God's reconciliation with man, hope, safe travel, and peace. A dove with an olive branch also represents the souls of those who have died in God's peace.

Noah, the ark, and the flood may be symbolized by a dove carrying an olive branch.

Palm

The palm represents the tree of life. Its branches symbolize victory and triumph over adversity. Martyrdom and immortality are also depicted by palm branches. When Christ is shown bearing a palm branch, the scene represents His triumphant entry into Jerusalem, His victory over death, and His martyrdom.

Thistle

The thistle and its thorns symbolize Christ's Passion, His crown of thorns, and earthly sorrow and sin. Saint Mary's thistle specifically represents the Virgin. (*See* Lion Background.)

BEFORE YOU START STITCHING, be sure your fabric or canvas is big enough. Use the stitch conversion chart on page 13 to find out how big the design will be on your material; then find the middle and start counting from the middle of the chart. Remember each symbol represents one stitch. Count, and count carefully!

Above all, enjoy the fascinating process of seeing the design emerge, stitch by stitch, from your blank surface.

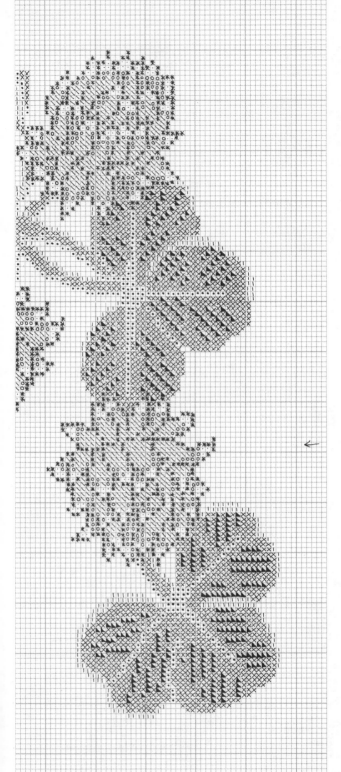

Clover

STITCH COUNTS

Horizontal/Vertical   190 x 185

SYMBOL	COLOR	PATERNAYAN PERSIAN #
◣	GARNET – V. DARK	920
•	GREEN – DARK	600
X	GREEN – MEDIUM	603
I	GREEN – LIGHT	326
·	WHITE	261
✳	PURPLE – DARK	310
\	PURPLE – MEDIUM	312
O	PURPLE – LIGHT	314

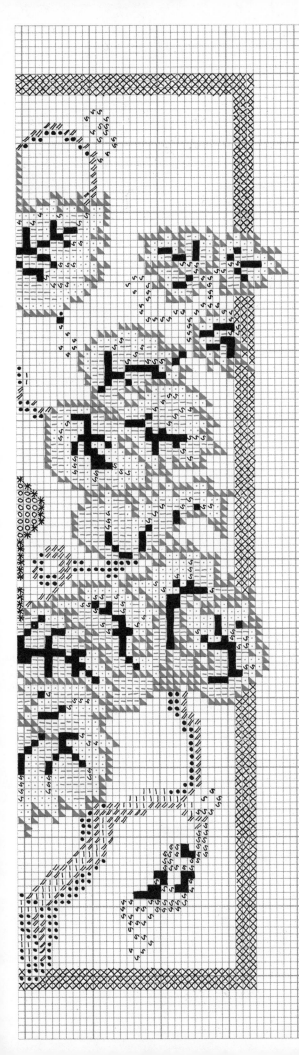

Grapes

STITCH COUNTS

Horizontal/Vertical   139 x 134

KEY

BLACK SYMBOLS		PATERN YAN #
l	BROWN – LIGHT	463
//	BROWN – MEDIUM	462
●	BROWN – DARK	460
+	PURPLE – LIGHT	324
O	PURPLE – MEDIUM	322
\	PURPLE – DARK	891
✳	PURPLE – VERY DARK	320
ς	COPPER – LIGHT	872
■	COPPER – DARK	870
X	SEA GREEN	532

GREEN SYMBOLS		
·	GREEN – LIGHT	653
–	GREEN – MEDIUM	652
◣	GREEN – DARK	650

Fir

STITCH COUNTS

Horizontal/Vertical   200 x 184

SYMBOL	COLOR	PATERNAYAN PERSIAN #
▶	GREEN – V. DARK	660
S	GREEN – DARK	661
X	GREEN – MEDIUM	662
O	GREEN – LIGHT	664
·	LIME – DARK	670
\	LIME – LIGHT	672
*	BROWN	740
+	GOLDEN BROWN	742
↑	YELLOW BROWN	744

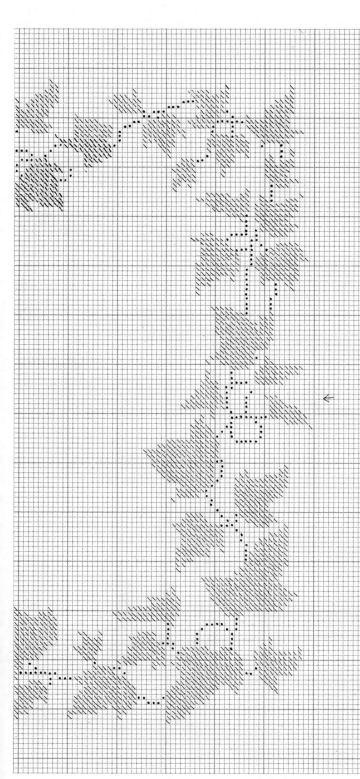

Ivy

STITCH COUNTS

Horizontal/Vertical   202 x 133

\	LIME GREEN	PATERNAYAN PERSIAN #	672
•	LIME GREEN - DARK	"	670

Olive and Latin Cross

STITCH COUNTS

Horizontal/Vertical   180 x 180

SYMBOL	COLOR	DMC FLOSS #
▶	BLACK AVOCADO GREEN	934
o	RED COPPER - DARK	918
X	SPORTSMANS FLESH	3064
•	KHAKI GREEN - DARK	3011
\	KHAKI GREEN - MEDIUM	3012
↑	FERN GREEN	522
S	FERN - LIGHT	524

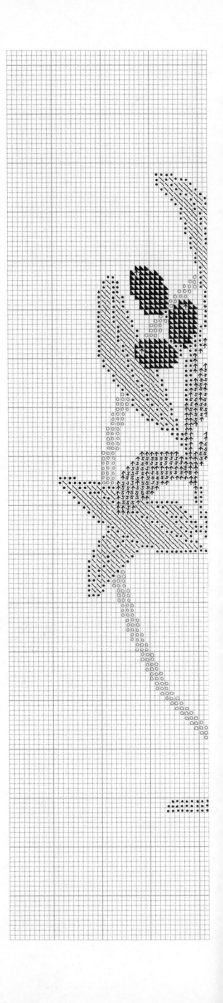

Palm

STITCH COUNTS

Horizontal/Vertical   210 x 130

STITCH COUNTS

Horizontal/Vertical   160 x 160

Bulrush

SYMBOL	COLOR	MEDICI #
X	DARK GREEN	417
↑	MEDIUM GREEN	418
−	LIGHT GREEN	419
■	BLACK	BLACK
✻	BROWN	306

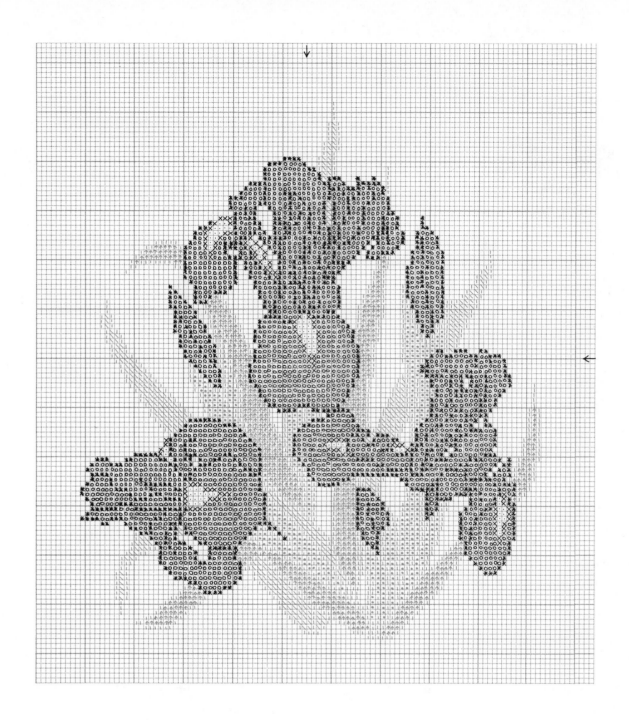

Iris

STITCH COUNTS

Horizontal/Vertical   120 x 110

SYMBOL	COLOR	DMC#
*	BLUE VIOLET — MED	340
o	BLUE VIOLET — LIGHT	341
×	TOPAZ — LIGHT	726
.	GOLDEN YELLOW — V. LIGHT	3078
•	HUNTER GREEN	3346
↑	YELLOW GREEN — MEDIUM	3347
\	AVOCADO GREEN — LIGHT	470
I	AVOCADO GREEN — ULTRA LIGHT	472

Lilies and Bee

STITCH COUNTS

Horizontal/Vertical   140 x 130

SYMBOL	COLOR	DMC #
.	WHITE	BLANC
◣	BLACK	310
×	TOPAZ — LIGHT	726
O	GOLDEN YELLOW — VERY LIGHT	3078
V	STEEL GREY — DARK	414
−	PEARL GREY	415
✳	RED COPPER — DARK	918
\	COPPER — MEDIUM	920
ꝫ	MAHOGANY — VERY LIGHT	402
+	SPORTSMAN FLESH — VERY LIGHT	951
•	HUNTER GREEN	3346
↑	YELLOW GREEN — MEDIUM	3347
I	AVOCADO GREEN — LIGHT	470
L	AVOCADO GREEN — ULTRA LIGHT	472

5

BORDERS AND BACKGROUNDS

Often the use of a border or decorative background can enhance a simple design. The following patterns come from Christian art and architecture and can be used for borders, boxing strips, luggage-rack straps, belts, bellpulls, table runners, and backgrounds. In some cases a single repeated shape makes up an overall pattern. At other times, several grouped designs provide an interesting interplay. A few of these motifs have Christian significance and can be used on their own or as complementary backgrounds.

When planning to use a border or background with another design, first compare the count in each chart to see that they are compatible in size. A small central design will be overwhelmed by a large background pattern, and a delicate border may look disproportionate around a bold central motif. When planning a boxing strip, remember that sides and top should be worked on the same count fabric or canvas. Also be sure that a finished boxing strip will not end up too long or too wide to later be sewn around the top. For long, narrow projects, decide in advance which way you want the stitches to lie when it's finished, and establish the top and bottom before stitching.

Stitch backgrounds and borders after you've completed at least the outline of the central motif so that you won't stitch into an area that another design will occupy. When combining designs, pull the colors of each in advance so that you may modify them if necessary.

Finally, consider using the following designs on their own for areas in which an understated or simple design may be the most attractive choice.

Aureole

The aureole is a brilliant area of light that seems to emerge in rays from the head or body of the Father, the Son, the Holy Ghost, or the Virgin, or representations of them. An aureole may be white, gold, or rainbow hued, and sometimes its rays end in the shapes of flames. It denotes supreme power and holiness.

Water

Water symbolizes the washing away of sin, renewal, purification, cleansing, and innocence.

In Baptism, water refers also to renewal. When used with wine in the Eucharist, it represents the humanity of Christ; wine, the divinity.

Scallop Shell

The scallop shell represents Saint James. When shown with droplets of water, it symbolizes Baptism.

BEFORE YOU START STITCHING, be sure your fabric or canvas is big enough. Use the stitch conversion chart on page 13 to find out how big the design will be on your material; then find the middle and start counting from the middle of the chart. Remember each symbol represents one stitch. Count, and count carefully!

Above all, enjoy the fascinating process of seeing the design emerge, stitch by stitch, from your blank surface.

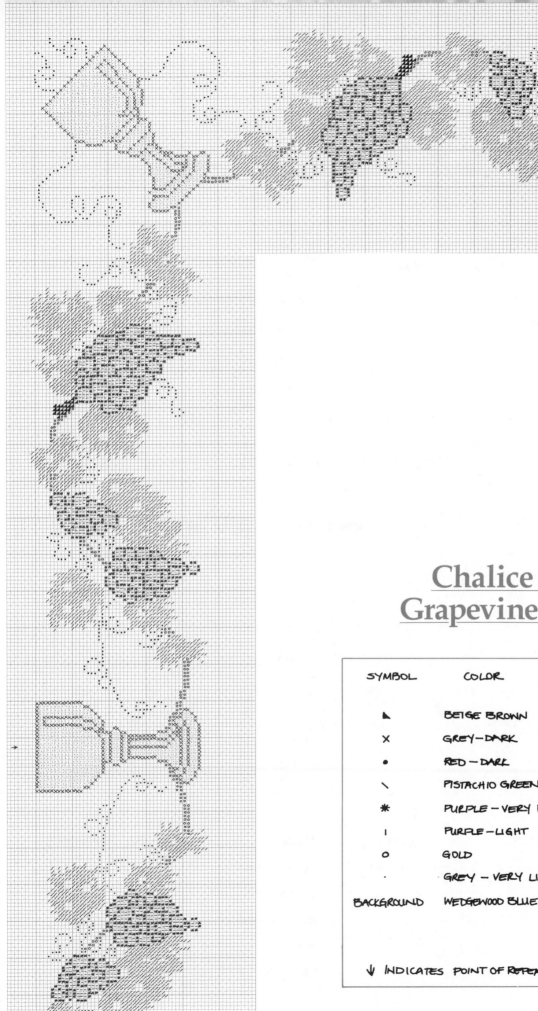

Chalice and
Grapevine Border

SYMBOL	COLOR	PATERNAYAN PERSIAN #
◣	BEIGE BROWN	472
X	GREY—DARK	202
•	RED — DARK	930
\	PISTACHIO GREEN— DARK	602
*	PURPLE — VERY DARK	295
I	PURPLE — LIGHT	322
O	GOLD	732
.	GREY — VERY LIGHT	246
BACKGROUND	WEDGEWOOD BLUE—DARK	072

↓ INDICATES POINT OF REPEAT IN DESIGN

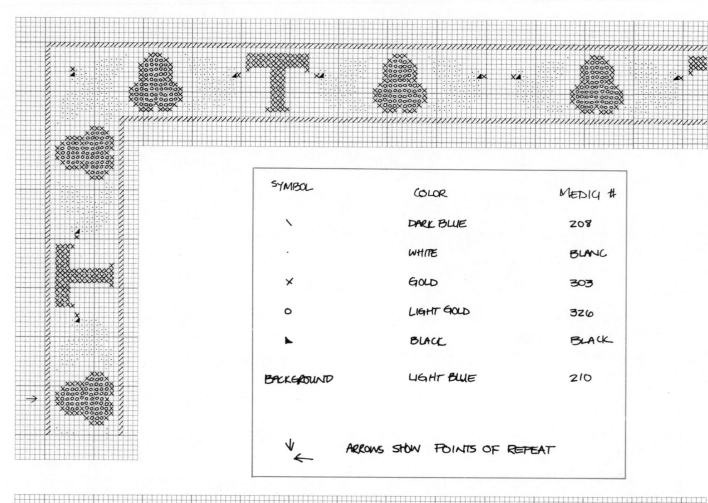

SYMBOL	COLOR	MEDICY #
\	DARK BLUE	208
.	WHITE	BLANC
×	GOLD	303
o	LIGHT GOLD	326
▶	BLACK	BLACK
BACKGROUND	LIGHT BLUE	210

ARROWS SHOW POINTS OF REPEAT

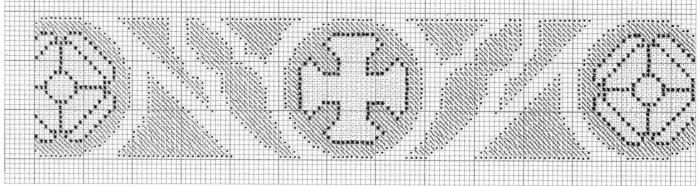

Border From Woodcarving

SYMBOL	COLOR	PATERNAYAN PERSIAN #
BACKGROUND	BLUE-DARK	501
•	BURGUNDY	901
\	RED-DARK	840
*	GOLD	732
.	GOLD-V. LIGHT	754

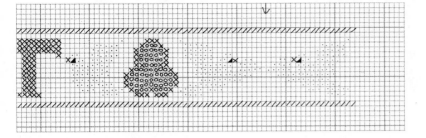

Dove Border

Olive Border

SYMBOL	COLOR	DMC FLOSS #
\	COPPER	918
•	BLACK/GREEN	934
×	DK. GREEN	3011
O	GREEN	3012

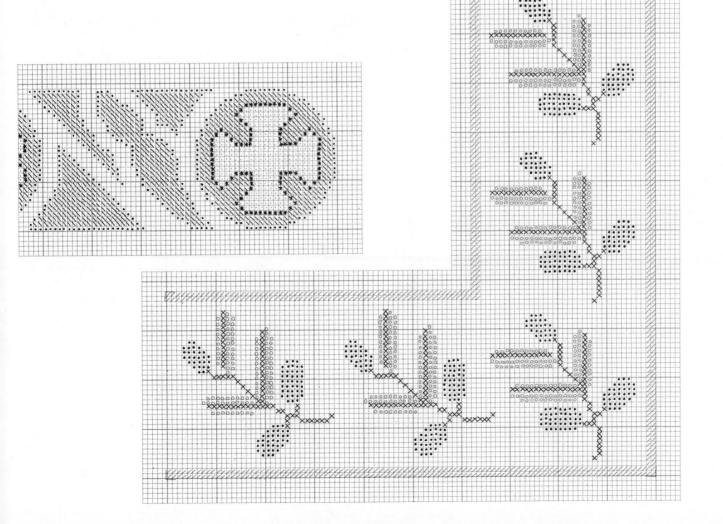

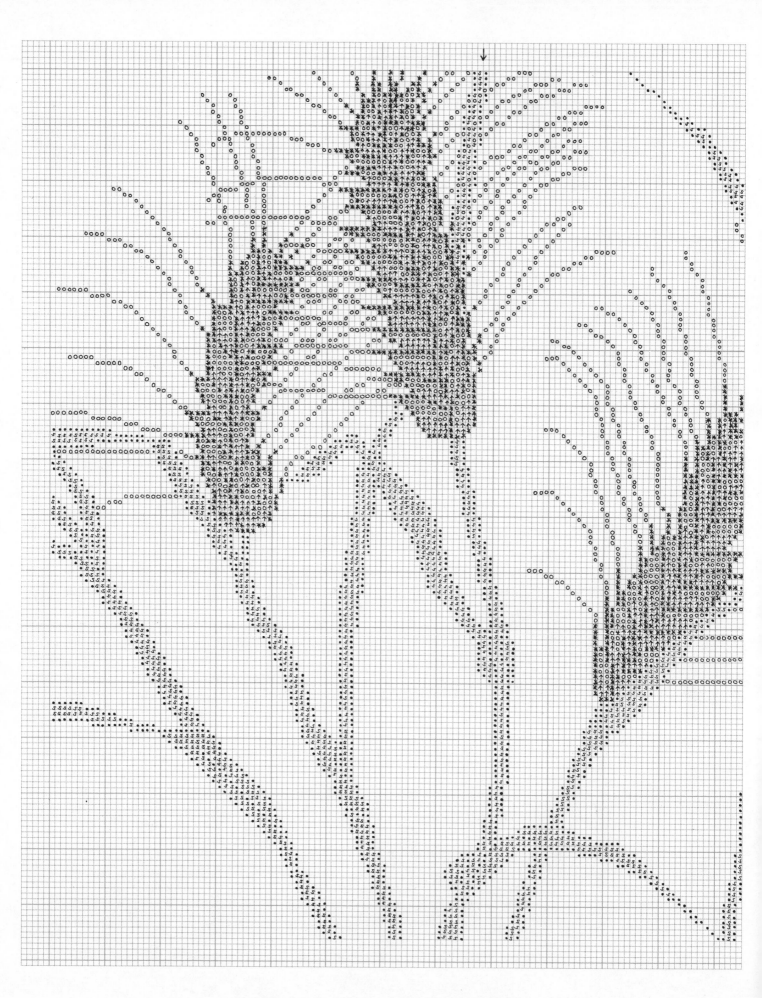

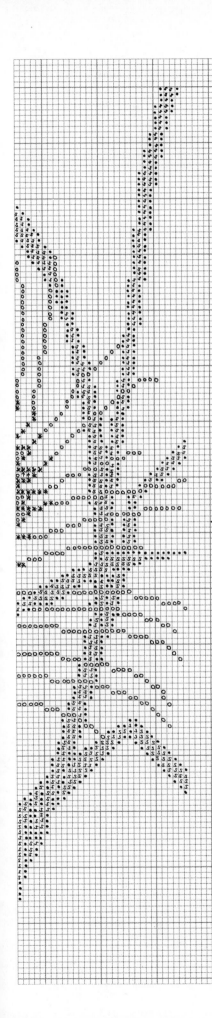

Grain

STITCH COUNTS

Horizontal/Vertical   156 x 156

SYMBOL	COLOR	MEDICI #
*	HAZELNUT BROWN	323
↑	OLD GOLD	325
o	GOLDEN YELLOW – LIGHT	7748
•	AVOCADO GREEN – MEDIUM	402
s	AVOCADO GREEN – LIGHT	420

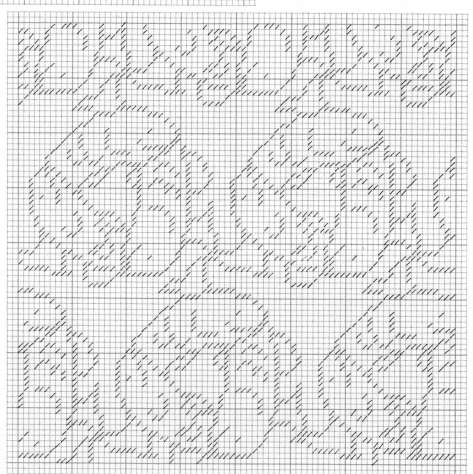

<u>Three-Fish</u>
<u>Background</u>

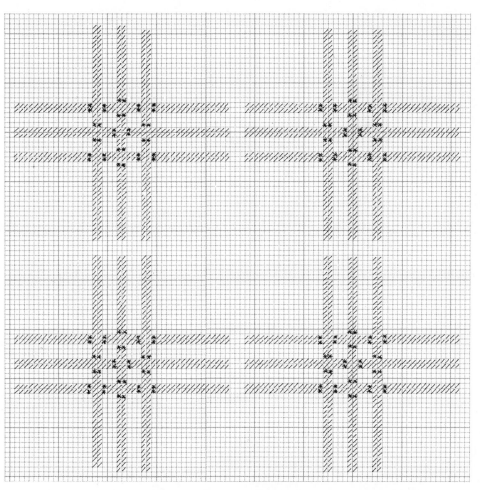

Triparted Cross Background

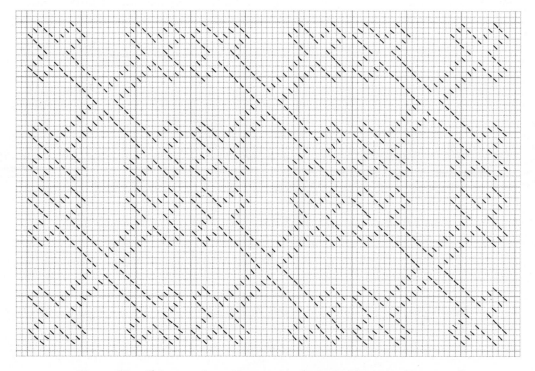

St. Julian's Cross Background

BIBLIOGRAPHY

Abrams, Richard I., and Warner A. Hutchinson. *An Illustrated Life of Jesus*. Nashville: Abingdon Press, 1982.

Ambuter, Carolyn. *Carolyn Ambuter's Complete Book of Needlepoint*. New York: Thomas Y. Crowell Co., 1972.

Dillenberger, Jane. *Style and Content in Christian Art*. New York: Abingdon Press, 1965.

Eaton, Jan. *The Complete Stitch Encyclopedia*. Woodbury, N.Y.: Barron's Educational Series, 1986.

Fenton, C. L., and H. B. Kitchen. *Animals That Help Us*. New York: The John Day Co., 1959.

Ferguson, G. W. *Signs and Symbols in Christian Art*. New York: Oxford University Press, 1954.

Freeman, Margaret B. *The Unicorn Tapestries*. New York: E. P. Dutton Inc., 1976.

Hulme, E. *Symbolism in Christian Art*. Poole, Dorset: Blandford Press Ltd., 1977.

Mitchell, Robert T., and Herbert S. Zim. *Butterflies and Moths*. Racine, Wis.: Western Publishing Co., 1977.

Rawson, J. *Animals in Art*. New York: Scribner Book Co., 1978.

Roels, I., and M. Koenig. *The Stork*. New York: Grosset & Dunlap, 1969.

Sargent, C. P. *Manual of the Trees of North America*. Vols. 1 & 2. New York: Dover Pubs., 1965.

Sill, Gertrude G. *Handbook of Symbols in Christian Art*. New York: Macmillan Pub., 1975.

Skrobucha, H., and H. P. Gerhard. *The World of Icons*. New York: Harper & Row Pubs., 1971.

Smith, William. *Smith's Bible Dictionary*. Philadelphia: A. J. Holman Company, n.d.

The Vatican Collection, as presented at the M. H. de Young Museum, San Francisco, CA, November 19, 1983–February 19, 1984.

Volbach, W. F. *Early Christian Art*. New York: Harry N. Abrams Inc., 1962.

Whitfield, P. *Macmillan Illustrated Animal Encyclopedia*. New York: Macmillan Pub., 1984.

Whittemore, Carroll E., ed. *Symbols of the Church*. Nashville: Abingdon Press, 1959.

INDEX